P9-CQI-254

RESEARCH IN MINISTRY

A Primer for the Doctor of Ministry Program

Revised Edition

By
WILLIAM R. MYERS

Introduction
by
W. Widick Schroeder

Exploration Press
Chicago, Illinois

Studies in Ministry and Parish Life

Exploration Press
Chicago Theological Seminary
5757 University Avenue
Chicago, Illinois 60637

ISBN: 0-913552-61-5

Library of Congress Catalog Card Number: 96-84945

ACKNOWLEDGEMENTS

Particular attention should be accorded the contributions of W. Widick Schroeder and Perry LeFevre regarding the formation and nurture of the Doctor of Ministry program of study at Chicago Theological Seminary, from which all examples in this book are taken. Notes about the contributors are found on pages 85-87.

This manuscript was ably critiqued by colleagues W. Widick Schroeder, Bonnie Miller-McLemore, Jack Seymour, George Cairns, and Mary Elizabeth Mullino Moore. While these folk helped me clarify certain points, the final responsibility for the manuscript is, of course, mine. A special word of thanks to my careful typist, Ms. Linda Parrish. Finally, I was introduced to both qualitative research and the case study method by my wife, Barbara Kimes Myers. Her friendly critique has kept me honest. I thank her for her presence and partnership.

William R. Myers

TABLE OF CONTENTS

Preface
to the Revised Edition

As a revised edition of *Research in Ministry* was discussed, it was decided to add several titles to the annotated bibliography, and to provide a preface. The core chapters of the new edition were to remain unchanged, in order that both the original and revised editions could be used simultaneously. Having recently written an article ("Keeping the Faith While Doing Research in Ministry") that presented the overall argument of this book, I suggested that essay could serve as the preface; my editor agreed and what follows as preface to the revised edition is that article.[1] W.R.M.

* * * * * *

All research methods, and there are many, are constructions. As constructions, the patterns of particular research methods are built upon certain assumptions about the world. These assumptions, and the research constructions generated by them, have ethical consequences. Research therefore is never a neutral activity; one engages in a particular research methodology in order to reach a "successful" and "useful" conclusion. What is or is not "useful" and "successful" must be determined by the researcher.

The researcher therefore makes a choice among research methods. For example, methods are often labeled *historic, philosophical, ethnographic, survey, case study, comparative, experimental,* and *quasi-experimental*.[2] If the researcher is a citizen of the United States, however, *research* usually is equated with quantitative, experimental or quasi-experimental methods. Such methods attempt to measure available data by the use of increasingly sophisticated statistical programs. In this method of research, controlled experiments are often set up in ways that isolate and attempt to measure contrasting sets of variables. True random samples (with equal opportunity for every item) and the clean delineation of experimental and control groups (with both submitted to pre- and post-testing) are essential components of this approach. Subjectivity on the part of the researcher is avoided; objectivity is sought. A "good" research proposal has a sample of sufficient size and clarity to be replicable; i.e., it can be run again and again. Control remains a critical factor for this kind of research, and theory is front-loaded; that is, a theoretical base must be fully considered before research occurs in order that the researcher can develop a hypothesis, identify variables, and propose an experiment.[3]

When a citizen of the United States considers doing research, it is this kind of research (quantitative, experimental, statistical) which is usually employed. The deep-seated acceptance of quantitative research as the norm in this country is a part of the broader culture's unbridled faith in enlightenment reason. Given the acceptance of this faith-stance, models of certainty are built from and made to depend upon "facts." Facts are employed to define progress in any arena. Knowledge thus becomes the sole property of science (and of verifiable, statistical, quantitative research); inside this culture scientific method and quantitative research have the power of unexamined dogma: "facts" equal truth and "facts" are understood to be identifiable via scientific method.[4]

Concern about the dominance of this research method and its underlying assumptions comes from at least two directions: (1) the question of *congruence* must be asked; i.e., is there a "goodness-of-fit" between the tools of the research method being employed and the project to be undertaken? For example, those who use the case study or the ethnographic approach to research question the facile transfer of tools and procedures borrowed from the natural sciences (such as agriculture) to the study of persons and of human affairs. They would argue that the quantitative research method can be most helpful in areas demanding control and replicable exactness, but that the same methods that can be employed to produce more bushels of corn per acre or put a man on the moon may not be useful or appropriate when considering the Civil War, a marriage, or a worship service at the little church down the street.

The second issue, however, is of more importance to the person of faith. It should be clear, these persons would argue, that this research method (quantitative, experimental, statistical) is not value-neutral. It is a kind of *faith system*. Born of the need to control and predict, this method honors objectivity and disavows subjectivity. Words like grace, transcendence, and God are not within its lexicon, precisely because they are suggestive of an alternative dynamic of change and truth. What is at stake here is more than exactness; the astute observer understands that wholehearted acceptance of this research method entails acceptance of a world-shaping paradigm in which clear lines have been drawn regarding what counts and is of value.

If the researcher is a person of faith (from whatever tradition), then the emergent question becomes "Can I embrace this research method without rejecting my faith?" This question is not grounded by a false naivete or in a simplistic rejection of things secular, but rather by the understanding that faith and research (or in my tradition, Gospel and research) are always in tension. A simplistic position for the one who believes is to reject or to distance oneself from the seductive lure of a particular research method. Neither this position nor the position which would simply conflate religion within a research paradigm appears to be satisfactory. As we enter a new century, we are uncomfortably aware of what happened in the last century when the language of faith was set aside and progress became equated with the instrumental use of reason.[5]

But can we move the other way? Can the researcher who is a person of faith adopt research tools *appropriate to the context of ministry* without collapsing into a sloppy imitation of certain tools of research? Can we take a step toward ministry that critically utilizes research without losing our soul? What follows in this book is a beginning move in that direction, but here I would emphasize two points.

First, ministry is not objective and dispassionate. But, for that matter, neither are research methods like the historical or the ethnographic. While at one time the historian firmly believed that it was possible to write an objective history and while at one time the anthropologist firmly believed that it was possible to convey the story of a culture without getting subjectively involved, neither method makes such claims today. The question for both the historian and the anthropologist is what and whose history, community, knowledge, and voice prevails in this account? It should therefore be possible to suggest to those engaged in ministry that research can occur even when the researcher is passionately engaged in the events being researched. And if the minister as the person of faith (or the historian or the anthropologist) attempts such research, then the story needs to be clear — this is *my* voice, these are *my* lenses, this is *one* descriptive account of what is taking place in this particular setting.

Again, this position is not new. The above paragraph could also sum up the therapist/client relationship. Most therapeutic research results in case studies of individuals or of systems involving neither random samples or sizeable populations (N usually =1). And most therapists reject as unhelpful any overly objective, dispassionate stance and expect that despite the power imbalance of their relationship with clients, they themselves will be changed/transformed (as well as the client) in therapeutic dialogue. Another way to name this process is to suggest that the therapeutic dialogue is a kind of on-going research project in which one or more persons are facilitated by a therapist who is engaged and is engaging in a process of transcendence. Thus the *case study* (in which N=1) becomes the research method of choice for many psychologists, psychiatrists, social workers, counselors and ministers. It begins to become clearer: the researcher who is engaged in ministry need not adapt to or accept a research method that distances or that reduces persons into bits of dispassionate data.

Another way to put this — the researcher who is faithful will begin to assume a pro-active research stance. The pro-active researcher, while philosophically occupying a more activist, transcending modality, borrows research tools from a variety of research methods in an effort to engage in "useful" research (and what is useful is not dispassionate or far removed from the context of the research). In such research, narrative descriptions (case studies) emerge in which researcher and participants are understood to be pro-active participants in the study. The case study therefore is a snapshot of an on-going process, not a static entity. Examples of pro-active research could be drawn from disciplines like psychotherapy (where "therapist" and "client" are understood to be jointly engaged in a transformative process), critical education (where the classroom is a "risky" place for student and teacher), or ministry (where the minister is "for" those who are engaged in the practices of discipleship). Research done within such professions primarily relies upon *observation, interviewing, journaling, the use of documents,* and the *telling of narrative story.* It is not coincidental that these skills also lie at the heart of professional ministerial training; i.e., persons who engage in professional ministry already utilize skills which in more formal and disciplined ways lie at the heart of research.

Nevertheless, the question of *congruence* re-emerges; "Is there a goodness of fit between a certain set of research tools and the project to be undertaken?" *Theory,* according to the translation of "theoria" by the theologian, Hugo Rahner, can be understood to mean "the vision of God."[6] Someone who accepts this understanding becomes engaged (as the human face of God) in a co-creative process. In part (and my second point), this assumption begins to define *good* (or "useful") research from *bad* (or "unuseful") research. The minister/researcher is called "to see what God intends or intended." While this admittedly is risky business, it is the way one connects to the ethical, to issues of justice, and of love and power. *Theory* in ministry therefore has to do with a communal awareness of those grounding assumptions warranting particular movement for God's reign, or toward "whole sight" in ministry. Those engaged in thoughtful ministry are expected to be able to see the pillars of fire and the clouds of smoke and to be able *to discern* — using certain skills — a way that leads through the wilderness. This is research for the believer, and it is accompanied by solitude, prayer, and communal worship. No one set of skills fits all circumstances, but those engaged in such pro-active faithful research will also regularly use interviews, assigned homework, field notes, critical instances from audio or video verbatims and sort through the found documents of a setting to hear the testimony of the community and to discern the tug or lure of the divine. And, if the concerns of the minister/researcher turn toward the inward journey of the researcher, then the use of a personal journal, a supervisory relationship, verbatims, and/or a regular focus meeting with a purposively chosen team or panel for shared reflection can be helpful in the process of discernment.

Validity in this on-going process is pursued by watching similar insight or testimony emerge through the use of several research tools. That is, when testimony of a similar sort appears through the use of three or more separate research tools, the researcher accepts that what is emerging is present in the ministry being observed. Validity, therefore, has to do with seeing in the final narrative description of the ministry (the case study) that which occurred in ministry.

Such case studies are important because they spark "naturalistic generalizations" on the part of their readers; that is, readers connect their own experiences to that of the case study and come away with a new perspective, insight or hunch regarding the role and the nature of ministry.[7]

It is the minister who seeks to share with peers a critical reflection from ministry who will seek a disciplined approach to the tools of pro-active research and who, after exploring the question of congruency, will come to rely upon either that evocative, tell-the-story skill (preaching) as it takes shape in narrative case study; or a mixture of other appropriate research methodologies.[8]

How D.Min. students sort out what the best research route might be for them is the subject of this book. It is written with the intended goal of being able to keep the faith while doing research in ministry.

End Notes

1. William R. Myers, "Keeping the Faith While Doing Research in Ministry." *The Journal of Pastoral Care* (1996) Vol. 50 (2), pp. 201-206. Reprinted with permission.
2. Richard M. Jaeger, ed. *Complementary Methods for Research in Education*. (Washington: American Educational Research Association, 1988).
3. W. James Popham and Kenneth A. Sirotnik. *Understanding Statistics in Education*. Itasca, IL: F.E. Peacock, 1992. If quantitative research is a mystery, this is a good book to orient the reader.
4. Numerous critiques of this position can be read. Of particular lucidity is Henry A. Giroux's *Theory and Resistance in Education: A Pedagogy for the Opposition* (New York: Bergens and Garvey, 1983).
5. I am referring to events as different as the Oppenhiemer Project in the U.S., and the rush by the church in Germany to side with Adolph Hitler.
6. Hugo Rahner. *Man at Play* (New York: Herder and Herder, 1965), pp. 28-29.
7. Robert Stake. "The Case Study in Social Inquiry" in *Educational Researcher* (1978) Vol. 7 (2), pp. 5-8.
8. Sharon B. Merriam. *Case Study Research in Education: A Qualitative Approach* (San Francisco: Jossey-Bass, 1991).

INTRODUCTION

In the past three decades, many North American theological institutions have developed Doctor of Ministry programs. Mixed motives were involved, for institutions sought to promote excellence in the practice of ministry, to provide a greater focus and depth to traditional continuing education programs, and to remain competitive in recruitment by catering to potential students' desires to earn a doctor's degree.

Many Doctor of Ministry programs incorporate a research paper as one of the requirements for the D. Min. degree. Some require a mini-thesis modeled after the academic doctorate, the degree which most seminary professors have earned. Informed by the idea of a legitimate distinction between an academic and a professional degree, other seminaries have sought to seek alternatives to the traditional research thesis as the culmination of the Doctor of Ministry program.

The Chicago Theological Seminary, which has had a professional doctoral program since 1967, has developed one alternative to the research thesis. Although this document usually includes a research component, the "professional paper," as it is called, is neither a dissertation nor a research paper. The author of the professional paper must address the implications of his/her findings for the practice of ministry. Each author seeks to reflect critically on some facet of ministry and to communicate his/her reflections to his/her professional colleagues.

William R. Myers draws illustratively from some of these professional papers to illumine the theory and research methods he discusses in this volume. By selecting illustrative materials drawn from substantive work, Myers is able to show how the theories and research methods he discusses are embodied in particular studies.

Myers recognizes that most D. Min. students have had little formal training in research methods and do not intend to become research specialists in one of the human sciences. At the same time they are interested in learning how the human sciences might illumine the practice of ministry.

In the development of Doctor of Ministry papers, students struggle with the definition of the problem in ministry they want to explore in their Doctor of Ministry projects. They also seek to formulate appropriate theory, to develop fitting research designs and to employ relevant research methods to study their problems. Drawing on his work with many Doctor of Ministry students, the author has skillfully shaped this text to address these issues.

Although he considers other research designs, in this volume the author promotes the case study approach to the study of ministerial practice. He also advocates a "pro-active" research method and qualitative studies, for he believes this approach helps one center one's work on issues focused in the practice of ministry. Whether or not one is persuaded by the author's theoretical viewpoint on these matters, in fact most Doctor of Ministry students will use the case study approach and often utilize qualitative research methods. Even if in principle they wanted to undertake elaborately designed causally oriented studies, they rarely have the resources to develop such studies.

The author's advocacy of case studies and qualitative research methods leads him to raise perennial issues dealing with the proper methods to study humankind. Although he does not address the roots of these methodological and substantive issues as they emerged in the late nineteenth and early twentieth century in Europe, he clearly prefers a "verstehen" (understanding) approach to socio-cultural analyses grounded in the German tradition and reflected in the work of seminal figures such as Wilhelm Dilthey and Max Weber. Weber, for example, held that human beings were meaning-seeking, meaning-positing creatures. Sociological study, therefore, entailed the study of the meanings and values which people hold and which are embodied in social structures. Because of the primacy of human decisions in social action, Weber thought one should seek to discern tendencies and configurations in the human sciences. He did not think the human sciences could or should expect to attain the degree of predictability possible in some of the natural sciences.

The author discusses the use of documents, questionnaires and interviews in doctor of ministry studies. In keeping with his preference for qualitative methods, he devotes substantial attention to the ethnographic method of research.

Whether he underestimates the a priori theory a person brings to ethnographic studies is moot. Regardless of one's views on the a priori character of some theory and some structural components, Myers addresses significant methodological issues and challenges rigid structural-functional modes of analysis and interpretation.

Exploration Press is pleased to offer this volume to persons who are seeking to develop their Doctor of Ministry projects. It offers thoughtful counsel and helpful suggestions to those who are in the process of developing their proposals. Its rich illustrative material helps the reader see the way theory, design, and research methods are embodied in particular studies. By exploring alternative designs and discussing various research methods, the text will help readers come to their own decisions about fitting theory, research designs and research methods to use in their own Doctor of Ministry projects.

W. Widick Schroeder

RESEARCH IN MINISTRY

CHAPTER ONE

STATING THE PROBLEM OR ISSUE IN THE PRACTICE OF A MINISTRY

The Doctor of Ministry course of study promises to challenge and nurture ministers regarding the practice of ministry. Because a practice of ministry encompasses so many things, many Doctor of Ministry programs demand that students concentrate this study of ministry within a definable area. The artificiality of such divisions often is overcome by the student's identifying an underlying issue or "problem" residing within the actual practice of a specific ministry. Once identified, this presenting issue is located within a broader "area" of ministry and usually frames coursework, the focus of peer reflection, the context of a project, the choice of an appropriate evaluative method for the collection of data, and the theoretical base to be used in critical reflection by the student. While some programs mandate several such explorations of ministry as "projects," others center the entire course of study around one such issue and the resulting critically-reflective paper. Regardless of the sequence employed, this book provides the Doctor of Ministry student with an understanding of how the tools of the researcher can aid in this process.

What, then, is understood by the phrase "a problem or issue in the practice of ministry"? Perhaps we can begin to understand this phrase by tuning into a fictive conversation with Judy as she visits her advisor following her Doctor of Ministry orientation.

The Entering Conversation

Judy entered the D.Min. program at her seminary as a way to critically reflect upon herself as a teaching and preaching pastor. While she had an intuitive sense of what she might focus on in the D.Min. program as a "problem in the practice of ministry," after the D.Min. orientation she quickly found herself in her new advisor's office.

Judy: I think of myself as a "teaching pastor," but I'm confused about what I might name as a "problem" in the practice of ministry.

Advisor: When you think of yourself as a teaching pastor, what concerns come to mind?

Judy: I'm troubled by children and their role in the church.

Advisor: One child? A group of children?

Judy: We've cut them off, at least in my church, from worship.

Advisor: O.K., let's play with that. What's the *problem* in the practice of ministry?

Judy: I'm troubled by the devaluation of children represented by the "children's sermon," but I'm not sure why. It's that we, and I mean my congregation, make no connection or room for the spiritual life of children within our worship! That's my *problem* in the practice of ministry!

Advisor: Yes. But you need to ask yourself if this really is your focus. You might discover instead, for example, that your issue or problem is with how adults view children who are involved in worship. You might then want to critically reflect on how adults relate to the presence of children in worship.

Judy: No. I think I really want to focus on how I can initiate a process in my congregation as we, including children, gather for worship.

Advisor: And at this point, you are clear enough to get started. Let's talk about how the course of study here might be used to help you get more clearly in touch with your practice of ministry.

*   *   *

CAUTION: At this point Judy seems somewhat clear regarding her "problem in the practice of ministry." Unfortunately, students like Judy often get stuck trying to clarify such specific "problems." Judy, while "somewhat" clear, is still not clear enough. That's what this book is about. We can, however, assume that Judy's D.Min. program will help her further clarify the specifics of this issue in her ministry. Judy's toughest yet most important step, therefore, is to arrive at a clear one-line statement of a specific problem in the practice of ministry that is researchable and, at the same time, manageable. It frequently helps to put the problem as a question. For example, given Judy's dialogue, her "problem" might be put like this: "How can I, the teaching pastor of a church, intentionally develop a helpful congregational process that includes children within Sunday morning worship?"

Using the "Problem" to
Initiate a Case Study

The chapters that follow in this manual pursue how D.Min. students like Judy can choose appropriate research tools and methods for the evaluation of intentional ministry. This manual suggests that a case study approach to the construction and evaluation of projects emerging from such ministries not only makes central those attitudes and skills normally underlying the practice of ministry (listening, observing, conversing, analyzing documents, critically reflecting, and story telling), but regularly accesses the kinds of data most frequently sought by D.Min. students.

A "case study" as a research process borrows tools from other research methods in order to focus holistically upon particular practices of ministry with persons, groups, programs, institutions, or systemic mixes of such components. The case study as a completed descriptive narrative (a "story") presents an example of ministry chosen from a natural setting and evaluated using appropriate tools that emphasize observations and interviewing skills as well as interpretations of documents. The case study, therefore, can be understood to interconnect *all* of the components being studied (the minister, problem, context, ministerial action, setting, individuals in that setting, theory, documents, and other data generated by "borrowed" research tools) within a single narrative paper. In this sense, a D.Min. case study offers the story of a careful documentation and a critical reflection upon a specific practice of ministry. Within this manual, the term "case study" therefore refers to (1) the case study process used to evaluate a specific practice of ministry, and (2) the eventual written description (the "story") of how that practice of ministry occurred and what it might mean. There is both a *process* orientation to the use of the case study approach (how one collects data), and a *product* orientation to the use of that same term (the resultant case study).

Written as a case study, the "end paper" of the D.Min. course of study can be a highly readable yet critically reflective document providing an interpretive framework that both informs and challenges the minister who reads it. What follows is the introduction to just such a case study in pastoral counseling by Ann Bartram. Her "area of ministry" is pastoral counseling; her "problem" or "issue" in the practice of ministry is the pastor-client sexual relationship. Entitled "A Response to Pastor-Client Sexual Relations," her initial page, reproduced below, serves as an engaging "hook" for those professional peers (in this case, pastoral counselors) who are considering the reading of her case study.[1] Bartram is "telling a story." Note how clearly she identifies her "problem in the practice of ministry."

A Response to Pastor-Client
Sexual Relations

by Ann Bartram

On a humid July day I was feeling hot, sticky and irritable as I saw clients on the hour. Why aren't ministers' offices air-conditioned? Coupled with these complaints were my own personal problems which had me feeling raw and fragile at that moment. Jayne, my three o'clock appointment, had just left and I opened the door to greet Tom, my last client for the day.

There he stood, one of my favorite and most interesting clients, looking the elegant jock he is, even in the July heat. White suit, pin stripe cream and brown shirt with coordinated brown silk tie, fresh from his air-conditioned car and his air-conditioned Bay Street office, he looked on top of life.

I caught his eyes and felt him take me in and as he did I saw his expression of concern. I leaned into the non-verbal communication and felt the vibrant electricity that is indescribable but unmistakable--the chemistry of sexual attraction flaring between us. I suppose I hoped what I was feeling hadn't happened, and I let it pass. Tom sat down and made to let it pass also. He began to talk very fast, straight out of his head, avoiding any eye contact with me.

What would I do? Would I call him on his behavior or ignore it? It had been in the air before this occurrence. It is my style as a counselor to call a person to what they are feeling. These thoughts flashed quickly through my head and I made my decision. "Tom, stop! What were you feeling just a moment ago when you came into my office?"

Tom stopped and grew very still. His eyes caught mine and flew away. Again the chemistry between us filled the room. "No way, Ann, I'm not going to tell you. Look, it makes my hands tremble to even consider it."

"Tom, I think that you had better say what you are feeling now. It is what there is." I speak softly, and I feel a mixture of excitement and fear. "Look, Ann, when I came in the door, you looked down, sort of hurting. (pause) I've never seen you like this before. (longer pause) I am really attracted to you, and I just want to hold you." Tom looked embarrassed and uncertain.

Inside me flashed the recognition of just how much I'd like to be held.
. . . .

This is a vignette from my personal case load as a specialist in pastoral counseling. It is presented as a graphic illustration of the presence of sexual feelings in a counseling hour. This is not an isolated occurrence.

Elsie came to me for help when she discovered that her pastor, who was counseling her, was having sexual relations not only with her but also with her friend and fellow parishioner.

Jenny was referred to me by the third male pastor from whom she had sought help. With the first two she had had intimate sexual relations.

A pastor came to me stricken with guilt because he was having sexual relations with a very fragile and hurting woman in his parish.

Such experiences as a pastoral counselor lead me to the seriousness of the question: "How will I respond to sexual feelings in myself, in my parishioner, in both of us, when and if they arise?" More questions follow in rapid succession as I attempt to answer this one question. Will I suppress, ignore, deny, avoid, and/or sublimate these feelings? Will I act or not act on them, and what will guide that decision? Will I allow them to be aired and explored as I would any other feeling arising in the counseling context?

*   *   *

Critical Reflection

Bartram's problem in the "practice of her ministry" as a pastoral counselor is very clear. She names it in a single sentence: "How will I respond to sexual feelings in myself, in my parishioner, in both of us, when and if they arise?" She makes use of the boundaries occasioned by the natural setting of her counseling office and her regular sessions with Tom, "one of my favorite and most interesting clients." The resulting introduction of her D.Min. paper defines the location of her case study (who, what, where, when, how, why). Within the body of the case study Bartram appropriately makes use of journal entries and verbatims taken from her audiotapes with Tom. On this introductory page, however, she has concentrated on identifying her "problem in the practice of ministry" in a way that produces an engaging "hook" for the Doctor of Ministry narrative description (the "case study") that will follow.

Thoughtful consideration of the professional literature and a clear conception of the meaning of pastoral counseling frames Bartram's case study. By the end of her paper, the theoretical implications are clear; we may agree or disagree, but they are clear. We can hunch, however, that because of Bartram's good use of evaluative tools as well as the story-telling expertise she displays, her peers will accord the case study she presents about her "problem in the practice of ministry" as authentic. They will connect with what she says, it could be argued, because it strikes them as congruent with their own experience in pastoral counseling. Her case study, therefore, confirms yet challenges the practices of ministry engaged in by her peers.

Summary

The identification of a "problem in the practice of ministry" is both the toughest and most important step that the D.Min. student must take. Such identification is helped by a clear location of the problem and its boundaries. Once located, the "problem" opens the way for the student to explore other tasks: for example, how relevant theory for a project is proposed, and how appropriate evaluative tools are chosen. The move from the identification of the "problem in the practice of ministry" to the writing of the final narrative description of the case study therefore spans the entirety of the D.Min. process.

Notes to Chapter One

1. Ann Bartram, "A Response to Pastor-Client Sexual Relations," in *Pastoral Care and Liberation Praxis*, ed. Perry LeFevre and W. Widick Schroeder (Chicago: Exploration Press, 1986).

CHAPTER TWO

NAMING THE CONTEXT OF THE PROBLEM IN THE PRACTICE OF MINISTRY

The movement from a broad concern (like the "place" of children in worship) to a specific practice of ministry (like introducing the active presence of children over six occasions in the Sunday worship of First Church, Middletown) is made clearer for both the D.Min. student and peers who may want to read a specific case study when the problem in the practice of ministry is clearly described in relation to the context in which that practice of ministry occurs. Context matters. And, because D.Min. case studies contribute to the ongoing exploration and understanding of ministry, peers who read case studies generated from D.Min. programs can only make generalizations to their own practice of ministry when the authors of such case studies clearly describe their contextual settings.

A Comparative Example: Simon and Brent

For example, Simon is a pastoral counselor who practices within a professional medical complex located near the university hospital in a large, urban setting. Simon sees many Asian-American couples in family therapy. Interested in the spiritual nature of therapy and well grounded in the so-called "Eastern" religions, Simon's speaking schedule keeps him from active participation in a local congregation.

Brent is also a pastoral counselor. Family therapy with Brent occurs in a set of rooms located within the church where Brent is a staff member. This Euro-American, lower middle-class, mid-size town church prides itself on nurturing family life. Brent can be seen either leading or actively participating in worship every Sunday morning, and he regularly suggests that families in therapy avail themselves of certain congregational activities, including what he calls "the spiritual discipline of worship."

Because of context, Simon's case study, while exploring the same problem in ministry as Brent's (the spiritual side of family therapy), will look quite different. And, without the presence of a clear contextual assessment within the paper, someone interested in the spiritual side of family therapy might be surprised at what Simon's case study suggests if they are left unaware of the context informing Simon's considerations.

Contextual Dimensions

In addition to helping someone who might read a particular case study, the adequate description of a context can help the student clarify the boundaries and the wide variety of issues undergirding a proposed ministry project. Dialogue with these issues can provide the D.Min. student with the sense of being fully grounded in the particularity of the chosen setting. D.Min. students are therefore encouraged to uncover and consider the implications of the context for their case study. At least four helpful, separate contextual assessments can be made.

1. *Demographic Assessment*. Demographics address categories relative to age, gender, marital status, socioeconomic status, race, ethnicity, educational level, etc. Demographics often appear on illustrative charts or graphs as numbers or percentages within a case study. Sometimes, however, a narrative description will do. An older, smaller, middle-class Episcopal congregation located within a rural, white, ninety-six percent Republican town is not the same as a younger, mid-sized, mixed-class, United Methodist congregation located within an urban, multi-ethnic, ninety-six percent Democratic city. A comparative chart built from demographic information can provide further data for such generalizations.

2. *Structural Analysis*. An analysis of a ministry's systemic structure uncovers and names the organizational model, either implicit or explicit, that most clearly describes the "shape" of the practice of ministry under observation. For example, if the D.Min. project is about youth ministry in a big church, it helps to know the systems that are both supportive and antagonistic to it within the church, as well as the structures outside the church that affect it--like the practices of social agencies, including the police, the school, and the merchants in the mall near the church. By uncovering such structures, the D.Min. student can become aware of power systems, leadership styles, and theological/denominational/ political choices that have been made.

3. *Historic Timelines*. The historic story provides us with the timeline of the ministry under discussion. For example, a social protest organized by an African-American pastor can take shape in a professional D.Min. paper with a periodization of the protest's "stages." Newspaper clippings, interviews, and the leader's personal journal can be used to document the journey of this particular

ministry from its initiation. By considering the factors involved in such historic timelines, D.Min. students often discover surprising implications for ministry.

4. *Symbols.* The symbolic factors, when named, often tell us a great deal about ministry. A simple question, "What's the story behind the bell tower?" can uncover much that had been previously missed. For example, one student who ministered in a small urban church noticed that the six previous pastors' pictures had been hung on one wall without any identification as to who they were or when they had served the church. When he asked one of the congregational leaders why no names or dates of the ministry of these men had been posted, he received this response: "If you need to ask, you don't belong here." Certainly "the previous pastors' pictures" were a symbol of how ingrown the church had become.

A Contextual Assessment

What follows is the contextual assessment made by Richard T. Kirchherr for his paper "Effective Preaching in an Era of Biblical Amnesia," a 1992 D.Min. professional paper for the Chicago Theological Seminary in the Chicago D.Min. in Preaching Program. Notice how this initial section of his paper summarizes the demographic context. Also notice how Kirchherr offers a structural analysis building on both theological (immanence) and theoretical (from Lyle Schaller) assumptions. Kirchherr also informs the reader about the church's history, paying particular attention to church attendance patterns as they inter-. act with the story of its preaching. This leads to a delightful comment on the symbolic role played by the pulpit in this particular church. By the time the reader concludes Kirchherr's section on context, the First Congregational Church (UCC) of Western Springs will be viewed as a unique and lively congregational expression and as a congregation the reader "knows."

The Context for the Thesis Project

by Richard T. Kirchherr
(used by permission)

To understand the context of the thesis work the reader should first have some answers to the question: Who are the persons who comprise the First Congregational Church (UCC) of Western Springs, and specifically, who are the persons of the thesis study? To answer this question it is appropriate to begin with some descriptive terms. The two that come to mind are homogeneity and diversity. Granted, these are words which would not normally be used to describe the same institution; however, in the case of the First Congregational Church (UCC) these seemingly opposite terms are appropriate in answering the question. The following glimpses and statistics will illumine this homogeneous church's pluralism.

A good place to begin, so as to grasp a basic understanding of this church, is with what seems common to its members. A visitor to the First Congregational Church on any given Sunday would be able to draw some immediate conclusions as to who this congregation is. "Upper middle class and all white" might be the first reaction of the visitor as she strolled up the church's front walk. Her second impression might be elicited by the architecture. "What a beautiful church building!" the visitor might think, and she would be correct. For the First Congregational Church was designed in 1929 (although the church was formed in 1887) by a well-known Prairie School architect, G. G. Elmslie. It is the only church he built, and it is a good example of Prairie School architecture. The horizontal nature of the sanctuary emphasizes the immanence of God's presence rather than the transcendence of God. In general, this fairly represents the theological perspective of many of this church's members.

Seated in the sanctuary for worship, the visitor might be deceived by the size of the congregation. She would find, on the average, 270 persons in attendance on most Sundays. That figure is low, according to Lyle Schaller, for a church which lists its membership at 1,400. (As an aside, the church is currently attempting to discern its actual membership, and by all estimates that number will be in the range of 1,000 to 1,100.)

Perhaps the visitor would be surprised by the number of staff persons listed on the back of the worship bulletin. She would find nine names on the program staff, three of whom are full-time clergy. That is a large staff for a 1,000-member church. The question might pop into the visitor's head, "How does a 1,000-member church support a staff of nine, a facility as large as this one, and an operating budget that is nearly $400,000?" The answer is that the average pledging unit's gift is almost $850. This is strong financial support. In a consultative paper, Schaller concluded that "By almost any standard this congregation enjoys exceptionally strong financial support."

If the visitor to the FCC were to interview persons in the pews she would discover several commonalities. A vast majority interviewed would have college degrees, and many would have attended graduate school. Related to the education issue, the visitor would find seated in the pews a preponderance of white collar professionals--not many doctors or corporation presidents, but quite a few engineers, lawyers, teachers, salespersons and managers.

Another commonality for this congregation is that the majority of women are not employed full-time in the workplace. Among those who are employed, most of their families could exist financially if they were not employed. Thus, in this community, when women work, normally they choose to do so for personal satisfaction rather than for financial reasons.

Stability is another descriptive word for this congregation. Almost one-half of the congregation joined the church before 1970. The average length of membership for suburban churches is ten to twelve years. Thus the figure of half of the FCC's members belonging for over 21 years is indicative of remarkable stability.

Politically, most of the persons in their pews could be described as "compassionate Republicans." Yet it is a community in which liberal voices are heard and respected, but one would not find many radical thinkers in the village. The community and the church are similar politically, economically, and racially. (Western Springs has only two black families out of a population of 13,500. The church has no minority members.) Thus, a visitor could conclude that the First Congregational Church is quite homogeneous, and she would be correct.

However, she would also be wrong. For the First Congregational Church is a changing congregation in some respects, and diversity (in the area of denominational tradition and theological perspective) is the result of these changes.

One of the reasons for this growing pluralism is that the church is no longer only a village church. Ten years ago virtually every member of this congregation lived in Western Springs. If one wanted to belong to a UCC church and one lived in Hinsdale or LaGrange (the two suburbs contiguous to Western Springs), one attended the UCC church in that town. Both of the neighboring villages have UCC congregations similar in size to Western Springs. A decade ago there was very little crossing of church boundaries. The environment is different today. People will travel up to twenty minutes to attend the church of their choice. The prevalence of the automobile is the main reason for the increased mobility of churchgoers. However, the second reason behind the changed environment is significant also.

Christians live in (and minister within) a consumer based society--a culture in which people are willing to comparison-shop for churches just as they would for a washer and dryer. People will travel to a church which meets their spiritual and/or familiar needs. Right or wrong, the area church, rather than the village church, is the reality in which the church ministers.

Supporting Schaller's belief in the idea of area churches rather than village churches is one more statistic from the FCC's new members. Of the last 125 new members who have joined the church in the past two years, over a third do not live in Western Springs. The congregation is becoming a 20-minute parish, and with these geographic changes has come another change.

This church is becoming quite diverse theologically. The vast majority of its new members are not from the UCC tradition. That unto itself is not particularly surprising; however, the number of former Catholics and non-mainline churches represented in the last two years' worth of membership classes is surprising. Approximately 40-50% of its new members (the total of which is 125, about 10% of the membership) is from the Catholic tradition, 10% from the Lutheran church, several Southern Baptists, Unitarians, Dutch Reformed, Episcopal, and even a family from the Mormon church have all joined FCC in the last 18 months. Perhaps one in ten had no affiliation with a church, and the remainder (about 25-40%) are from mainline traditions. This overall pattern appears to hold true for the last five to seven years of new members. The visitor to the First Congregational Church would initially observe a seemingly homogeneous congregation, but beneath the surface that visitor would discover a theologically heterogeneous community, and an increasingly denominationally pluralistic church.

One other piece of history that the reader should be aware of relates to the history of preaching in this congregation. It has long been expected that its senior minister exhibit strong skills in the pulpit (preaching has consistently been the focus of the senior minister's position in this church). Those pastors who were outstanding preachers are remembered for their skill, and those who were less than excellent are remembered for having been so. This expectation (although to a lesser degree) carries over to those who share pulpit time with the senior minister.

One architectural fact should also be noted. The pulpit is elevated and its design boxes the preacher into it. It has three wooden sides to it and the back is a wall. There is only one narrow stairway into and out of the pulpit. It is said that when the church was built, the minister at that time liked to pace as he preached. So the building committee told the architect to "box him in so that he'll stay in one place." Perhaps the story is apocryphal, but to this day the preacher in the First Congregational Church of Western Springs stands in one place when he (all male, to this point) preaches.

*   *   *

Summary

A concise assessment of the "problem in the practice of ministry's **context**" includes a careful analysis and review of (1) demographics, (2) structures, (3) timelines, and (4) symbols. By making visible the context of his ministry, Richard T. Kirchherr goes a long way toward helping the reader assign credibility to his resultant case study.

CHAPTER THREE

MAKING EXPLICIT THE THEORETICAL STANCE OF THE D.MIN. STUDENT

Once a presenting issue, question, or problem in the practice of ministry has been identified and contextually located, the D.Min. student is asked to make explicit an initial working theory as the student intentionally considers how to engage in ministry in this setting. It takes time to build theory, but by the time an end paper is presented in the D.Min. course of study, the theoretical framework hopefully has come together; for example, in a D.Min. paper entitled "Grief and Mourning," Rabbi Gary Gerson quickly names his theoretical assumptions and clarifies how they inform his case study about ministry:

Grief and Mourning

by Gary Gerson

The purpose of this paper is two-fold: it offers both a new theory of the funeral and a model of how that theory may be implemented. The theory is predicated on three assumptions. First, that grief is experienced and expressed by bereaved family systems as well as by bereaved individuals. Second, that the ritual process characteristic of funerals in traditional and preliterate society serves to promote empathy and consequently grief work by the family and a sense of transformation and growth. Third, that the one who has died may be evoked as a presence in memory. As this presence is made real in family dialogue and is confirmed in the eulogy, it acts as a co-joining and mediating agency. This agency confers power, meaning and grace for the work of grieving, reconciling, and accommodating to mutual needs.

* * *

Gerson indicates that he will revisit these theoretical assumptions in greater detail. Not only will the case study be interwoven with critical implications from these theoretical assumptions about ministry, but Gerson's ongoing immersion in rites-of-passage literature will also come to the fore. In this way, Gerson's D.Min. paper can be understood as an interactive case study about grief and mourning in the Jewish tradition.

The Interactive Nature of Theory

Since theory can be named before the project, develop in conjunction with the project, and also emerge out of data gathered from the project (depending on the research method; see chapter four), students sometimes struggle with over-zealous attempts to make their "theory" too explicit too early in the D.Min. process. Nevertheless, while theory and its construction can appropriately be encouraged at any time through a variety of factors in the D.Min. process (course work, specific sequential ministry projects, conversations with peers, clinical training, consultations with advisors, paying attention to the spiritual disciplines, and personal growth), a case study approach to research suggests that it is important to begin naming whatever theory is present in the mind of the researcher at the earliest possible moment in the D.Min. process.

While the student's initial theory about a specific problem in the practice of ministry is, therefore, often at best tentative and is certainly open to reformulation, struggling to name it at the earliest possible moment in the D.Min. process both accents and complements whatever theory will emerge as the student engages in evaluating the data gathered throughout the case study. This is both the perspective of case study research and of ministry; the minister engages in a collaborative, dialogical, reflective, interactive process. Theory emerges in tandem with practice instead of in a "top-down" authoritative model. The D.Min. process therefore asks students to name, as best they can, and as early in the process as they can (while remaining open to future "learnings"), the theoretical "hunches" they are using to inform possible ministerial action(s) that might occur within a given project.

The Informing Theory of One Case Study

Felix Sugirtharaj's D.Min. paper concerning "The Liberation of Harijans in South Indian Villages" is a good example of a narrative case study in which an intuitively held theory can be said to have played an early initiating role.[2] The first page of his case study is reprinted following the next paragraph of this chapter. As you read it, note how Sugirtharaj's informing theoretical ideas are buried within his introduction: he passionately seeks a "new language" in the "transformation" of the "socio-political" world in which "unjust structures" remain unchanged. This intentional activity is something to be lived, claims Sugirtharaj, and will be seen, he asserts, in his D.Min. case study of a youthful group of Christians in India.

While Sugirtharaj's comments are neither sufficiently integrated or complex to be called, on this early page of his paper, a fully developed theory, note how certain categories can be abstracted from his introduction. Four categories emerge that theoretically inform his approach to the ministry project: (1) his own *experience* as an untouchable, (2) the Christian missionary *tradition*, which he will not discount, (3) the importance of the *scriptural message* for Sugirtharaj, and (4) the *reasonable methods* of community organization that should be used, according to Sugirtharaj, in community transformation. He suggests that much of what he claims will be borne out in his case study, and while one might agree or disagree with the initial components of Sugirtharaj's theoretical position, the reader has been given a clear indication of where the author of this case study theoretically "stands."

The Liberation of Harijans
in South Indian Villages

by Felix Sugirtharaj

This paper is addressed to those people who are speaking of a new language to redefine the reality in which they live and who are seeking to critically analyze the socio-political situation which keeps the unjust structures unchanged. If they happen to read this paper, they will understand that it is not simply a theory, based on some optimistic ideology, but a true and lively story which is being experienced by a group of committed young people in the typically oppressive rural context of India.

The message is that faith in humankind, faith in the future of man and of all people must be sustained. Let it be reviewed on the basis of what is taking place in the political life of our country today.

Who Am I? I am by birth an untouchable—a Harijan. I was born and raised in a small untouchable village in South India. My relatives are still uneducated, primitive, backward, and extremely poor. I am thankful to the missionary movements which brought soup, soap, and salvation to a large number of Harijans in Tamil Nadu. Since my grandparents became Christians, the missionaries agreed to put me in Christian mission schools and colleges for education. I am one of those few who have been richly benefitted by the Christian missionary activities in India.

I am also an ordained minister. I believe in Jesus Christ and His salvation. The Bible teaches that liberation of people involves historical projection for the creation of a new man and a new social solidarity. In relation to my faith, liberation is freedom *from* bondage and freedom *for* love and fellowship with God and all men. Therefore, hatred, misery, suffering, poverty, hopelessness, and discrimination are not any longer laid at the door of fate or superstition, but on men who are responsible for the society. My stance is not to physically convert others into Christianity or to claim that Christianity is the only religion that has the answer to all the Harijan problems, but to witness to the righteousness and justice of God in the liberation of my fellow-men at whatever risk may be involved. From 1965-1973, I worked among slum dwellers in the city of Madras. With the cooperation of other social welfare organizations, a team of us tried new techniques, including community organization, to build up a strong, powerful force to tackle social issues.

* * *

Naming Theory

D.Min. students like Sugirtharaj sometimes approach the theory-naming process by considering the presence or absence of four categories: reason, scripture, experience, and tradition. While there is nothing magical about the use of these four categories, and many will recognize therein the "Wesley Quadrilateral," some such correlative process should occur (for example, using the work of persons like David Tracy, James D. and Evelyn Whitehead, or Paul Tillich). This chapter suggests that when named categories such as these four (tradition, experience, reason, scripture) overlap, interpenetrate, and confront one another, they can help make explicit the often intuitive theoretical place in which the minister stands.

1. *Tradition.* Whom do we claim as our "cloud of witnesses"? If, for example, the Roman Catholic tradition is the church within which "I" stand, while I can certainly learn from other traditions, the problem I am exploring in the practice of ministry will become more explicit as it interacts with or is placed in correlation with the Roman Catholic tradition. And this may mean that I need to become familiar with those areas of my tradition (or other traditions) that might provide necessary or alternative forms of guidance for my task. "Tradition" also includes the broader historic and current traditions of theological reflection, including figures far removed from a person's denominational placement, but nonetheless relevant. "Dialogue partners" chosen with this category in mind could span the centuries, yet readily can be seen to inform each other as well as the D.Min. project (for example, a consideration of the "dynamics of sin" in Augustine, Calvin, and Reuther). In any case, no theory regarding the practice of ministry can avoid the claims of tradition.

2. *Experience.* Humans come to knowledge via experience. This is the primary source for questions or concerns in the practice of ministry. In that senso-

ry experience involves the personal participation of the knower, "my" (our) experience is of worth. Ministry, therefore, is based in part on such experiential knowing, and because of experience I/we know more than I/we realize in relation to the problem under consideration. Given this framework, as experience is placed in correlation with the problem, I/we may be triggered with the memory of certain experiences, and may need to spend time introspectively "getting in touch" with this rich area. This is where "my" voice is listened for; "I" am in dialogue with "myself." Spending introspective journaling time in correlation with the problem faced by me in ministry can be highly productive. But note that in this section I occasionally have used plural pronouns in order to suggest that a communal voice may also need to be heard into speech. Again, any theory held for a particular project must connect with an experiential sense of what makes a particular ministry valid.

3. *Reason.* While not seeking to provide a rationalistic conception for ministry, depthful ministry ought to be reasonable. All theory involves reason, and reason involves much that goes on in what we sometimes call "secular" disciplines. The D.Min. student should assume that persons in these disciplines have already considered some of the factors involved in the "problems" under consideration by most D.Min. students. A literature search within the appropriate disciplines (psychology, anthropology, education, etc.) should provide the student with the state of any ongoing discussion. As with the section entitled "Tradition," the use of reason implies another set of dialogue partners (for example, in education, Dewey, Freire, and Apple). Placing the ministry issue side by side with the way the issue is discussed by the "voices" in such disciplines ultimately calls for an in-depth theoretical correlation.

4. *Scripture.* In the Christian tradition, "scripture" refers to what is commonly called the "Old" and "New" Testaments. The reformers understood these scriptures as the most valued category used to judge all other categories; i.e., scripture alone (*sola scriptura*). But there are other "scriptures" . . . the Koran, the Gita, etc. The D.Min. process may ask how/if the scriptures associated with "my" tradition impact, judge, or are of no consequence to the "problem" under study in the practice of ministry. The correlation carried on here ought to be at least as specific as was suggested for the previous categories; the Gospel of Luke, for example, is not the same as the Gospel of Mark. Again, any theory that avoids the claim of scripture must make a case as to why this area has no words of worth regarding someone's "practice of ministry."

Beginning Correlations: Examples

As categories like these four overlap and are correlated with one another's claims, they in turn are interpenetrated by the problem and the emerging ministry action(s) contemplated by the minister. Gradually, a theory can be constructed. In this fashion, all D.Min. students are encouraged to become more intentional, more critically reflective, and more explicit regarding what it is that they think they are doing theoretically in their "practices of ministry."

Because D.Min. programs press students toward such theoretical clarity, there necessarily emerge within such programs a multiplicity of theoretical stances; i.e., no two persons ever hold the same identical position regarding the practice of ministry. Nevertheless, since students in ministry often are intuitive and have difficulty being explicit about theory, one helpful way to assess the adequacy of any student's theory is to ask, "How does the student correlate reason, scripture, experience, and tradition with the ministerial practice(s) contemplated in the D.Min. project?" For example, consider the following theoretical patterns as they begin to unfold in the work of three separate students.

1. Cameron's "problem" centers on preaching. He feels he has been locked for too long within manuscript preaching (this is his experience). He is exploring a theory of preaching which centers on storytelling (he is reading about this in homiletical theory; we could call this the category of reason). He has traced the storytelling done by two early preachers within his own denominational heritage (tradition), and he is considering doing a project in this area utilizing certain parables from the New Testament (scripture). He believes the four categories are equally critical as his theoretical stance begins to emerge regarding his problem in the practice of ministry.

2. Ralphetta's "problem" is located within Christian education. Making her theoretical stance explicit involves her wrestling with how the A.M.E. church interprets the Sunday School movement (tradition); the use of the Bible in that process (scripture); anthropological understandings regarding the role of oral communication (reason); and her personal pilgrimage within a local A.M.E. congregation (experience). While believing she has a lot to learn regarding theories of oral communication (reason), she personally ranks the four categories in the following most- to least-valued sequence: (1) experience, (2) tradition, (3) scripture, (4) reason.

3. Menson's "problem" is identified with the grief process within pastoral counseling. Making explicit Menson's theoretical stance involves a deep commitment on his part to Jungian theory (reason), and clinical experience gained from his personal pastoral counseling practice (experience). For Menson, insights emerging from these two categories clearly blend together into his explicit stance "for" ministry. He is less clear as to how (or if) tradition and scripture inform that stance. Perhaps these are areas of ministerial and theoretical growth for Menson.

Summary

Thus, while D.Min. students necessarily understand the relative worth of categories such as these four (tradition, experience, reason, scripture) in a variety of ways, the insights gained as students struggle with such categories are helpful in clarifying the theoretical frameworks they will use regarding particular problems in ministry.

Notes to Chapter Three

1. Gary Gerson, "Grief and Mourning," in *Pastoral Care and Liberation Praxis*, ed. Perry LeFevre and W. Widick Schroeder (Chicago: Exploration Press, 1986).
2. Felix Sugirtharaj, "The Liberation of Harijans in South Indian Villages," in *Pastoral Care and Liberation Praxis*, ed. Perry LeFevre and W. Widick Schroeder (Chicago: Exploration Press, 1986).

CHAPTER FOUR

DISCERNING APPROPRIATE RESEARCH METHODS FOR D.MIN. EVALUATION

Thus far we have taken a look at the problem (chapter one), its context (chapter two), and the role theory plays in the projected practice of ministry (chapter three). We have now arrived at a point from which we can begin to reflect on how D.Min. students can choose appropriate research methods in order to critically evaluate projects (their "practice") in ministry.

The choosing of a particular research method sets the D.Min. student (wittingly or unwittingly) upon a course in which the outcome, in terms of the kind of data generated, is already predetermined to a stronger degree than what the student anticipated or cares to admit. Such research methods have been developed from a variety of needs: (1) the quantitative research method hopes to *control* by discovering objective proof, (2) the ethnographic research method hopes to *understand* by describing the meaning of certain contexts, and (3) the pro-active research method hopes to *transform* individual and collective settings. In the following pages, these three research methods will be considered.

1. The Quantitative Research Method

A quantitative method attempts to measure available data through a sequence of increasingly sophisticated statistical programs. In this method of research, controlled experiments are often set up in ways that attempt to isolate and measure contrasting sets of variables. Key to such measurement is a true random sample (with equal opportunity for every item) and the identification of experimental and control groups with both submitted to pre- and post-testing. Subjectivity on the part of the researcher is avoided; objectivity is sought. A clean design has a sample of sufficient size and can be seen to be replicable; i.e., it can be run again and again. Control remains a critical factor throughout this kind of research, and theory is front-loaded; that is, a theoretical base must be fully considered *before* research occurs in order that the researcher can develop a hypothesis, identify variables, and propose an experiment.

While it is assumed by many that this is the best way to do research, it is also recognized that the serendipitous moment occasionally turns what was perceived to be an experiment's "glitch" into pure gold. While one does not expect to see a quantitative case study (case studies are not engaged in "control"), the case study approach to research often borrows and uses quantitative tools from this method because they are often helpful in gathering particular kinds of data. For example, chapter two suggests that quantitative demographic data must be collected and analyzed in order to clearly understand the contextual setting of ministry. In similar fashion, other tools are often borrowed from the quantitative approach and used in case studies, but few D.Min. students sufficiently share the values regarding control and predictability underlying this approach to fully place their project's evaluation within this research method. Fewer still have adequate resources (numbers, money, time, research staff) to begin the kind of projects envisioned. Nevertheless, certain D.Min. ministry projects can appropriately use tools borrowed from this method, and persons who wish to function entirely within this method should check resources other than this book for any amplification of appropriate quantitative tools.

A good example of how a case study approach might "borrow" a quantitative research tool is Bonnie Niswander's D.Min. paper, "Initiating Congregational Rebuilding Through the House Church."[1]

Initiating Congregational Building Through the House Church

by Bonnie Niswander

This article is a progress report on the impact of a house church experience which constituted the first segment of a larger project of community rebuilding and faith stimulation within a local congregation. . . .

In an attempt to measure and evaluate the results of the project, questionnaires were administered to participants in the project at three successive stages, and to non-participatory members who thus served as a control group. . . . . . . on the basis of preliminary findings, together with written and oral evaluations by the participants, I hope to show that the House Church was valuable and effective. . . .

* * *

Niswander moves through a historic description of the practice of ministry she is observing, but eventually returns to the question of evaluation.

In order to assess as completely and as accurately as possible the effects of the house church and the seminar which followed, both written subjective evaluations and questionnaires with scaled items of the Likert-type were used, supplemented by a final oral group evaluation and some additional brief interviews. Initial brief-form questionnaires (containing 38 items) were completed by House Church participants before the weekend began, relating to religious and personal feelings and attitudes. After the house church weekend and prior to the beginning of the seminar, both the house church and the additional seminar participants completed longer questionnaires, which repeated the items on the first questionnaire and included additional questions on personal data, and attitudes concerning the ministry and activities of the local congregation and broader religious issues. After the seminar, all participants (both groups) again completed the long questionnaire, so that changes occurring through the successive experiences could be calculated and compared. In addition, one half of the congregational members (both active and inactive) who did not participate received the same long questionnaire before the seminar began, and the other half of each group received it afterwards--thus serving as control groups, as well as providing additional data on the congregation as a whole. In addition, house church participants responded in writing to six questions on a "reflection sheet" following the weekend experience, and seminar participants completed a nine-question evaluation following that experience. A final oral evaluation session including all house church participants and small-group leaders closed the project.

*　　*　　*

Niswander is careful about how she reports data gathered from her use of these primarily quantitative tools.

Although verification of the validity and reliability of the statistical data is not complete, preliminary tabulations show a consistent positive shift of mean scores on items relating to religious and personal feelings and attitudes which do tend to corroborate the participants' reports of heightened awareness and appreciation of the church as a supportive community, of increased confidence in their leadership ability and satisfaction in its experience, of growing willingness to trust, of deepening faith and greater appreciation of the Bible as a useful resource for living.

*　　*　　*

Again, while tools from the quantitative research method can and will be borrowed for case study research, it should be understood that resources other than this book should be checked for appropriate quantitative procedures (see annotated Bibliography).

2. The Ethnographic Research Method

The ethnographic research method sets out to describe what can be seen by someone (usually described as an "outsider") who wants to understand what is going on within a culture or a subculture (such as the youth group in a particular church). In such research the researcher becomes a "participant/observer," i.e., the researcher steps into the culture as someone from outside the culture who nevertheless is attempting to uncover that culture's meaning. Critical to such research are those persons from within the system who are "gatekeepers" (persons who assure access), "key informants" (persons from inside the culture whose words are trusted by the researcher), and the disciplined use of subjective, personally generated data from the researcher's own perspective (via a personal journal, field notes, verbatims of supervisory sessions, etc.). "Good" ethnographic research assumes that data gathered from three dissimilar sources (triangulation) can indicate the emergence of a "generative theme," yet submits such interpretation to critical review from both insiders and outsiders, incorporating their suggestions as part of any final descriptive picture. Theory is more of a "back-loading" process; i.e., the core of what comes to be understood as "theory" emerges and is grounded out of the ethnographic process as it connects with the culture under study. A weakness of this style of research therefore occurs when a researcher cannot identify personal assumptions and theoretical biases. While ethnographic case study replicability is low, researchers assume that a good ethnographic study will rate high in validity; i.e., it adequately will describe (like a snapshot) what is actually going on at a particular moment within a culture.

John Chalmers, a Roman Catholic priest from Australia, spent two years in Chicago observing and critiquing a seminary pastoral formation program.[2] Chalmers uses ethnographic tools in his paper and does so from the interested stance of an observer who will return to Australia and his own pastoral formation program. His paper is entitled "Completing the Task of Seminary Pastoral Formation: The Transition from Seminary to Parish"; in this excerpt, Chalmers tells the reader about his research method.

The Transition Program Assessed by its Participants

by John Chalmers

In assessing the Transition Program I used a triangulation method to gain access to the experience and considered reflections of its significant players. I sought the history and documentation of the development of the program. From twelve key informants who had participated in the program since the mid-1980s I sought considered reflections and suggestions about areas of the program needing further work. From the current class-in-transition I sought a glimpse of what it is like to be a newly-ordained priest in his first parish.

* * *

Note Chalmers' claim of "triangulation." This involved his use of purposive interviews developed from two historically significant pools, plus extensive use of program-generated documents. In that Chalmers is an "outsider" studying the practice of someone else's ministry, Chalmers claims his research method as "ethnographic" and approaches that method as one who will write a "narrative description" (a "case study") about a Pastoral Formation Program.

Many D.Min. students feel comfortable with the values and the tools undergirding this method, but find time constraints and the amount of data produced to be somewhat daunting. A certain level of uninvolvement and "distance" on the theoretical side of the method seemingly makes it more user-friendly for professional researchers than for ministers. But, if one can study ministry in settings other than one's own, the ethnographic method makes good sense for the D.Min. program. Some D.Min. students will therefore use this method as an entry point from which they will choose a complex of appropriate evaluative tools for their D.Min. research component. The tools that are central to this method will be presented in chapters six through eight.

3. The Pro-Active Research Method

The pro-active research method intentionally engages in qualitative research while pro-actively working toward transformation. In this method the researcher is passionately involved with the practice being evaluated. In such research, narrative descriptions (case studies) emerge in which researcher and participants are named as pro-active participants in the study. Examples could be drawn from disciplines like psychotherapy (where "therapist" and "client" are understood to be jointly engaged in a transformative process), pro-active education (where the classroom is a "risky" place for student and teacher), or ministry (where the minister is "for" those who are engaged in practices of discipleship). Research done within such professions primarily relies upon observation, interviewing, journaling, and the use of documents. It is not coincidental that these skills also lie at the heart of ministerial training. Such research usually results in the presentation of a narrative description (a case study). Tools are often chosen for use in this research process on the basis that they can be entered into by both the therapist and the client; for example, both the client and the therapist might keep personal dream journals from which the client reflects with the therapist, and the therapist critically reflects with a supervisor on both client- and therapist-generated dreams. When the larger community becomes engaged in such pro-active research, tools may also be "borrowed" from the quantitative research method, as well as others; for example, documentary or philosophic methods. In one sense, however, whether dealing with individual or communal transformation, it is the interview that becomes this method's primary tool of assessment (see chapter seven).

Note that data is gathered from not only the participants and the setting, but also honors subjective material generated by the researcher. Because the researcher's generation of subjective data is also valued, the personal journal of the researcher often becomes central to the data gathering process, primarily because pro-active research places high priority on naming and monitoring such personal factors in an effort to ground and make theory more explicit (see chapter eight). Regardless of the complex of research tools chosen by the researcher, however, theory is interactive, emerging not before the period of research, but in conjunction with it. Research tools that can capture this dynamic process are necessary if this research method is to "work."

A weakness of this method is the sometimes strident nature of its reporting; i.e., a continuing posture of advocacy sometimes overwhelms data with little sense of truth remaining. When pro-active research is done well, however, the reader engages in what is called a naturalistic generalization, a term used in both method two and in this method to describe how such descriptions, once read, spark comparative responses out of the reader's own experience. Pro-active research underlies articles, for example, like "Becoming a Spiritual Director for the Homosexually Oriented Candidate for the Priesthood in the Roman Catholic Tradition of Celibacy" by Thomas J. Byrne.[3] After introducing the paper, Byrne suggests a subheading:

Catch 22: Doing Things Differently

by Thomas J. Byrne

I am currently the spiritual director for some homosexually oriented candidates for the priesthood in the Roman Catholic tradition of celibacy. Their stories are an experience of oppression. The seeming "exclusion" of their very persons from ordained ministry because they are "disordered" and "inclined toward intrinsic evil" is an interpretation of tragic proportions. The hostile homophobic environment, a paranoia surrounding AIDS, and multiple pedophilia lawsuits involving priests creates the context for pastoral care of these candidates.

*   *   *

Note the tone of Byrne's work. Also note the theory he brings to his ministry:

I envision spiritual direction as a *ritual* of the "liminal experience," a passage, as it were, in self-understanding from a living "in the closet," through a special bonding "betwixt and between" in spiritual direction itself, and a return to everyday life with a new understanding, a new *hermeneutic* of the orientation which sees it as a gift of God, not a curse, with a special gospel mission to the whole community of church.

This has been my experience. I want to share it with you. First, I need to make more explicit my theoretical framework. Then, I will offer an illustrative case study. Finally, I need to raise some problems and promises inherent in this ministry.

I have paid close attention to my experience as a spiritual director, and I consulted a dozen others who are currently involved in the formation of candidates for the priesthood.

*   *   *

As Byrne shares his theory of liminality and spiritual direction, he also makes his claim: "This has been my experience. I want to share it with you." He is going to do this through an "illustrative case study." That study will make use of his personal journal and twelve purposive, open-ended interviews with spiritual directors like himself. He will also purposively interview persons under his care. He will, in addition, utilize the documents of the Roman Catholic Church in order to provide a framework for his experience. We can see that he is engaging in a pro-active research method, and that his approach to this method is that of the case study. Many D.Min. students will adopt a similar complex of tools as they position themselves within the pro-active case study research method; its primary tools are presented in chapters six through eight.

Critical Reflection on the Three Methods

The quantitative research paradigm (method #1) was birthed through instrumental, scientific reason and a static conception of the world. Quantitative researchers seek the objective facts of phenomena with little or no interest in the subjective world of individuals. In contrast, instead of seeking to control and predict, the ethnographic research paradigm (method #2) seeks to describe and come to understand the meaning of human behavior in a "strange" setting outside the researchers's own frame of reference. Those who use qualitative paradigms (such as the ethnographic) question the facile transfer of tools and procedures borrowed from the natural sciences (such as agriculture) to the study of human affairs. But the pro-active research method (method #3) goes further than the ethnographic method's attempt at description--instead of describing or understanding a phenomenon, it seeks to *stand with* the persons in the phenomenon, even as the phenomenon and the persons involved experience the process of transformation. The pro-active researcher, therefore, intentionally and actively engages in the experience that is being researched.

On the face of it, this third research method--the pro-active--is radically different from methods one and two and sounds congruent with those implications of transformation most closely associated with Judeo-Christian conceptions of ministry. It more clearly fits, for example, the theological claims made by most Doctor of Ministry programs.

Pragmatically, however, the advocacy stance of our third category--a research method that is pro-active, positively emphasizes the subjective involvement of the researcher, promotes community interaction as a part of all research, and seeks "critical transformation" as a grounding premise--tends to put the D.Min. program that accepts it at odds with many or most contemporary Western research traditions (and, concomitantly, with research method #1, the quantitative method, the one most seminary Ph.D. professors were trained in using).

In addition, like most seminary professors, the majority of D.Min. students are American. Because of this they can be said to have a singular interest in what can be called "the instrumental use of reason"; i.e., they want to wed theory and practice in such a way that, through evaluation, via a method like #1, they can *control* how something "works." This utilitarian picture rings true in many areas of ministry today. The minister, whether chaplain, pastoral counselor, religious educator, parish administrator, or youth worker, is first and foremost a "professional"--a "hired gun" or "expert" who "is competent" and "has the tools" to "do ministry." This can also be an overlay of methods #2 and #3. While this subverts the philosophic underpinnings of methods #2 and #3 and misses most of the religious grounding of ministry, many D.Min. students (and professors) nevertheless continue to succumb to such underlying beliefs about their programs and the appropriate role research should play within them.

Summary

Viewed in this more comprehensive fashion, where the values of a given research method are understood to play a formative role in the ministry research project, it becomes clear that a casual approach on the part of either the student or the professor in the choosing of a research method (from methods one, two, or three) may result in a toxic decision for the D.Min. project. What seems essential is that a critical assessment of both the researcher's and the research method's values regarding a particular practice of ministry be made. Both student and professor must therefore recognize that all research methods (including the pro-active "third" method) have value-laden, pragmatic consequences for ministry. Those who choose a given method should therefore not be surprised at the kinds of data that emerge. In addition, given the impact of any research method upon the practice of ministry, professors involved in teaching research to doctoral students might benefit by understanding such teaching as one of encouraging discernment in order that ministers might come to choose appropriate tools for doing research within ministry. In the understanding of teaching espoused in this chapter, the professor, therefore, is called to be more like a "spiritual director" of a "formative process" than like someone who has been hired to simply teach a "statistics course."

Notes to Chapter Four

1. Bonnie Niswander, "Initiating Congregational Rebuilding Through the House Church," in *Spiritual Nurture and Congregational Development*, ed. Perry LeFevre and W. Widick Schroeder (Chicago: Exploration Press, 1984).
2. John Chalmers, "Completing the Task of Seminary Pastoral Formation: The Transition from Seminary to Parish," in *Creative Ministries in Contemporary Christianity* ed. Perry LeFevre and W. Widick Schroeder (Chicago: Exploration Press, 1991).
3. Thomas J. Byrne, "Becoming a Spiritual Director for the Homosexually Oriented Candidate for the Priesthood in the Roman Catholic Tradition of Celibacy," in *Creative Ministries in Contemporary Christianity*, ed. Perry LeFevre and W. Widick Schroeder (Chicago: Exploration Press, 1991).

CHAPTER FIVE

THE PRACTICE OF MINISTRY AND THE PROJECT PROPOSAL

Once a problem in ministry has been contextually located, an initiating theory identified, and an appropriate research method chosen, the D.Min. student turns toward formulating a "project" for engaging in "the practice of ministry." Perhaps we can begin to better understand what is meant by this phrase by returning to our fictive conversation with Judy, the pastor mentioned in chapter one, whose "problem" in the practice of ministry had to do with the exclusion of children from her congregation's weekly Sunday worship.

Judy: I think I can name my problem and I think I can locate it within my congregation, but I'm not certain what is meant by the practice of ministry.

Advisor: Judy, what you do as a pastor about this problem is your practice of ministry.

Judy: So if I begin a process that eventuates in my congregation's experiencing children in Sunday worship, that whole process could be understood to be my practice of ministry? And this process could be my D.Min. "project?"

Advisor: The simple answer is "yes," but a more complex response will really push you to define intentionally the "who, how, where, when, and why" of that process, along with the "what."

*   *   *

The Project Proposal

While Judy's conversation helps us begin to understand what might be meant as her "practice of ministry," it also suggests that intentionality on the part of the minister concerning ministry is highly valued in the D.Min. process. Not that foggy notions about ministry are unimportant, for they often hide or cover perceptions and assumptions, but such "fog" needs to be dispelled in advance of a D.Min. project. A "project proposal" clearly spells out what acts of ministry will occur, with whom and where they will occur, and why the minister is choosing to minister in just this way (and not another). A simple outline of a "project proposal" might include the following:

1. State the problem in the practice of ministry;
2. Name the context of this problem;
3. Describe the contemplated practice of ministry;
4. Make a coherent statement regarding the theory informing this practice of ministry;
5. Name the research method that will be used to critically evaluate the resultant practice of ministry (what are the tools congruent with this method that will be used);
6. Include a brief bibliography;
7. Note the course-of-study taken (courses, seminars, workshops) that help define the particulars of this project.

*   *   *

"Project proposals" that follow this or similar outlines force D.Min. students to clearly consider the specific components of any projected "practice of ministry." So it is that Judy quickly finds herself in a peer consultation regarding her proposed "project."

Judy: My project is to observe and evaluate what happens in the worship service at my church next year as I attempt to involve children in that worship.

Neil: Judy, I'm not clear as to whether your focus is children, the adults, the political process, or the changes you experience as a minister during this process.

Arlis: And I'm wondering, Judy, just how you intend to keep track of a year's worth of Sundays, the overlay of the political process, and the way all this affects the children. Is all this clear to you? Or, are you doing too much?

*   *   *

A good Doctor of Ministry project proposal, despite the many pitfalls surrounding it, is an attempt on the part of the minister to outline the component parts of an intentional plan, a kind of architectural blueprint, though necessarily open to adaptation, by which a specific "practice of ministry" can be located, engaged in, observed, described, and evaluated. A lot of thought and conversation with peers in ministry must take place in order to achieve such a clearly stated project proposal. Consideration, therefore, must be given by the student in the project proposal to mundane factors such as *time* ("how many weeks or months or years is the project going to run?"), *money* ("perhaps you should interview all three hundred persons, but can you pay folk to type all the responses gathered through such a task?"), and *appropriateness* ("will the people be willing to be interviewed, and what happens if the church won't agree to this project?").

As Judy considered the numerous facets of her project, she quickly rewrote her initial proposal; several weeks later she returned to another peer consultation.

Judy: In a nutshell, I want to do a case study of one congregation's experiment regarding children in worship. This is a two-year project. It will occur in my congregation. I will engage appropriate committees and boards in year one. My goal is congregational approval of an intentional experiment for year two. That year-long experiment will center upon the presence of children in worship.

Neil: I'm still curious about your focus, Judy. Is it the process, the kids, or your own journey?

Judy: I'm saying that my problem (the absence of children in worship) can only be addressed by a leadership process within the whole church structure that involves me as minister. My board supports me in this project.

Arlis: I think you need to be very clear on your focus. It sounds to me like you are the focus, and that worship leadership is your area. Am I right?

* * *

Judy has reached a somewhat satisfactory identification regarding her "practice of ministry." She can expect, however, that her project proposal will be further pushed by her peers and advisors toward even more clarity regarding not only her intentional ministerial practice but also the theoretical ideas she brings to the project and the evaluative tools she wants to use in this project.

Four Challenging Questions

In preparation for a subsequent conversation regarding her project proposal with her D.Min. advisor, Judy was asked to answer four provocative questions:

1. What *audience* will this paper impact? (Judy mentally defined her audience as pastors, religious educators, and persons interested in liturgy.)
2. Can the *implicit thesis* of the author be made explicit? Stated another way: What "hunch" does the author hold about this project? Or what is the author's hoped for "good news"? (Judy knew she had a "politi-

cal" agenda here. Because of baptism, she believed all who had been baptized were members of the church, regardless of age, and that no child should be excluded from worship in "the household of God.")

3. Are the project's *theories connected to a named discipline/body of research*? Is there a working bibliography? Has a literature search occurred? (Judy was fully informed on the latest books, articles, and current thought pertaining to worship involving children because of two courses taken in the previous academic year.)

4. Are the theories of this project also integrated and consistent with the author's *theological position* in ministry? (Judy was an advocate who sought, in this project, congregational transformation. She affirmed incarnational theology. For Judy, worship was where the people of God make their response to God's presence. She was also a pastor who felt she had the trust of her congregation, and she believed she had their support for a project such as this one.)

*   *   *

Judy came away from her advisor's office with the growing sense that through her project's emerging guidelines she could assume that her practice of ministry (her leadership at this moment in her congregation) would become clearer to her. She explained this point to a friend in the following way: "I'm doing a case study, and while I have some informing theoretical ideas about what might happen as I engage the congregation along certain lines, I fully expect that I will have more questions (and more theoretical ideas) by the end of my project than when I began." And Judy is correct in her assessment. Case study research does not begin with a fully realized theory about the practice of ministry from which a researcher proves or disproves certain variables; case study research takes certain informing ideas about ministerial practice and, working in natural circumstances (like within Judy's congregation), engages those ideas toward the formulation of a more spirited and coherent practice.

Given her case study approach to evaluation, Judy recognized that her proposal, therefore, also had to include evaluative tools appropriate to her project. She was particularly certain that whatever tools she would use had to be unobtrusive and yet had to be also related to the world of her congregation in ways that neither overwhelmed the children or antagonized the adults. Her advisor had one word of advice: "Remember that your project--that is, your intentional practice of ministry--is the focus, not the research component." Judy translated this to mean that a certain research tool was "appropriate" when it helped her acquire usable and trustworthy data for the story that was quickly becoming her case study.

The Project Proposal: An Example

What follows is an attempt to look at how a project proposal was incorporated on the part of Avis Clendenen within her end paper in order to inform her readers about how her case study was initiated. "Reconstructing Religious Education: A Model of Challenge in Applying the Feminist Critique to the Teaching of Religion" is an insider's pro-active account of one Roman Catholic high school religious department's attempt to revise curriculum.[1]

Method of Study

by Avis Clendenen

In order to elicit the most objective and broad based insights into both the nature of the curricular changes and the process of setting new departmental directions, all fifteen faculty of the Religion Department were requested to confidentially answer the following questions:
1. In your recollection what factors prompted the re-examination of the religion curriculum?
2. How would you describe the intent behind and the purpose of the curricular revision?
3. Is it a fair assessment to say that the new religion curriculum has been influenced by the feminist critique of the Judeo-Christian tradition?
4. What is the source(s) of your enthusiasm for this venture?
5. What concerns, limitations, dangers would you identify as facing you in particular, or the department faculty as a whole, in continuing to advance the theological content and educational methods begun through this new curriculum?

A seventy-three percent return was received to this written request.

The method of study also included a review of all department meeting minutes that recorded the year-long development of the new curriculum. The North Central Secondary School Association Evaluation Reports on Mother McAuley High School were valuable in providing an historical sense of the need for this revisioning of the religion curriculum. The philosophy of both the school and the department provided a backdrop to the motivating assumptions of McAuley High School. The 1979 National Bishops Catechetical paper, *Sharing the Light of Faith,* along with Marianne Sawicki's *Faith and Sexism,* provided the necessary context in which to do an analysis of contemporary American Catholic catechesis.

Three key interviews also enriched the scope and quality of the findings. The interviewees included the past chairperson of the department who served at McAuley for nine years and left the school prior to the implementation of the revised program of study; the present chairperson who has served at McAuley for eight years and has major responsibility for implementing the new program; and the senior faculty member in the department with fourteen years of service in the religion program at McAuley. Each of these interviews lasted between one and one-half and two hours and each interviewee was asked to respond to the following inquiries:

1. Summarize the mission of the religious education program at McAuley.
2. What is your working definition of feminism? Tell me how you see the impact of feminism on the Roman Catholic tradition, its theology, and American Catholic religious education?
3. How is teaching a ministry for a Catholic religious educator?
4. What are the strengths of the curricular revision for both the students and the department faculty?
5. What concerns do you have or do you hear from others regarding a Catholic secondary school religion program incorporating or reincorporating women, the female, the feminine into Christian/ Catholic history, religious language, scripture study, liturgy, etc.?

The findings to be presented here could be extremely helpful for others in the profession who may be anticipating a similar undertaking, or trying to support the necessity of revising their religious program to reflect the fuller reincorporation of women to the core curriculum of Christian catechesis.

*   *   *

Notice Clendenen's use of a variety of research "tools" in her year-long effort to collect usable data for the case study. These included (1) a confidential, written questionnaire (see chapter seven), (2) a review of all department meeting minutes (see chapter six on "documents"), (3) the use of two "approved" papers to do documentary analysis (see chapters six and seven), and (4) three purposive, thematic interviews (see chapter seven). Also note that her theory relies upon a feminist base that included Marianne Sawicki's controversial paper, *Faith and Sexism* (see chapter four). Clendenen also brought an "insiders" perspective, often relying upon "field notes" (see chapter six).

While Clendenen's case study cannot be reproduced in full for this chapter, it is clear that her project proposal worked to her advantage, for in it she clearly had identified her problem, the contextual location of her ministry, an intentional direction for her practice of ministry, a rich theory, congruent evaluative tools, a pro-active research method, and an appropriate narrative case study format. Clarity at the project proposal stage regarding these key components appears to have been critical for her successful completion of the D.Min. course of study.

Summary

The project proposal determines a plan by which the student can enter a setting usefully, using appropriate evaluative tools while remaining aware of the ongoing importance of theory without closing down critical implications for the practice of ministry discovered in the ongoing process. Without such a plan, the Doctor of Ministry student is lost. With such a plan, the student can be open to the transforming moment, secure in the knowledge that the boundaries of the project have been agreed upon by both Advisor and the Doctor of Ministry Committee.

Notes to Chapter Five

1. Avis Clendenen, "Reconstructing Religious Education: A Model of Challenge in Applying the Feminist Critique to the Teaching of Religion," in *Creative Ministries in Contemporary Christianity*, ed. Perry LeFevre and W. Widick Schroeder (Chicago: Exploration Press, 1991).

CHAPTER SIX

GENERATING DATA FROM THE SETTING

The case study "tells a story" about ministry for our time. The story that is told may or may not be perceived as being trustworthy, in large part because of the disciplined use, or lack, of appropriate research tools. While many such tools exist, certain tools can be said to do a particular task better than others. Often such tools can be used within research methods that are called, for example, quantitative, ethnographic, or pro-active (chapter four). Still other methods, not presented in chapter four (for example, philosophical or historical) can be used in order to provide additional tools for research. A requirement for the usage of certain research methods and/or tools, therefore, seems to be knowing what kind of data is being sought by the D.Min. student. One way to ask the question about the appropriate choice of research tools is to recognize that differing kinds of data can be generated from three broadly defined areas (or "domains"): (1) the *setting*, (2) the *participants* in the setting, and (3) the *person of the researcher*.

Students, depending on the particular demands of their project, may wind up using three tools that collect data from only the setting. Other students, given their peculiar needs, might choose only one tool from this chapter (or no tools from this chapter). Again, the question of what complex of tools could/should be used is answered in large part by the kind of data that the researcher needs to access. While some project might receive ample data from the use of only one tool, other projects may require two or more tools.

Because this chapter describes the D.Min. researcher collecting data from *the setting*, it will consider three research tools: (1) field notes, (2) audio/videotapes, and (3) "found" documents. In that theological education emphasizes the ability of the minister to observe, interview, and critically reflect upon documents, these three research tools seem particularly congruent for evaluating ministerial "practice."

1. Field Notes as a Way to Generate
Data from the Setting

Field notes are written, typed, or taped observations made by the D.Min. student concerning what has occurred in specific settings within the context of the D.Min. student's project. A particular D.Min. student may make such note-taking a public activity. Another D.Min. student may decide that the act of taking such notes while remaining in the setting does not fit with what normally goes on in a given ministerial context, and may, therefore, not take notes but follow each observation with a disciplined and detailed later written recounting of what had earlier been observed. Still another D.Min. student (who has excellent word-processor skills) might audiotape field notes while driving home; upon arrival home, the student might spend an additional hour or two at the word-processor, transcribing the audiotape into a set of written "field notes." Such field notes often look like this:

(today's date, setting, time of day)

I am sitting in a sanctuary one-half hour before First United Methodist's Sunday worship. The sanctuary was built in 1924. The heavy wooden beams are in the McCormick House style (with painted rust, gold, and green design). There is an altar rail, and the focus of the room is the pulpit, which stands directly in the center of the front third of the sanctuary. The communion table, smaller than expected, is located in front of the pulpit in a lower perspective and is partially blocked by the communion rail. The pews are narrow, cushions tilt the congregant toward the front, but the pews are not built for comfort. The pews curl around the pulpit. The choir, backed by a big pipe organ, will sit behind the pulpit. There are red carpet runners. The baptistry is located in a corner, almost out of sight. There are no flags (American or Christian) in sight. At 15 minutes before the service a janitor moves the baptistry into sight, filling it with water. As he concludes his task, he uses some of the water to brush back an errant lock of hair.

*   *   *

Project proposals usually state the occasions during which such field notes will be taken. A given project proposal, therefore, might propose that field notes be the major assessment tool, because the student is going to be following the historic development of ministry in a particular group over a specific time span. In this case, field notes might be used to record developmental progressions, and could be taken during the formal occasions when the group meets. In addition, two or three "special occasions" might be anticipated during which extra field note-taking should also occur. If anticipated, these "extra" occasions are also named as part of the project proposal.

Because the intent of taking such notes in the field is to collect data that will aid the author in writing a descriptive narrative or "case study" of a given ministerial experience, field notes are often used because they have the advantage of capturing what is going on in a given setting at a specific moment. In taking such notes the student describes the setting (see above), perhaps by including a sketch of how objects and people are arranged. But in addition, because such field notes also include the activities and interactions that occur in a setting, the attention of the researcher is also paid to all kinds of things, including the frequency and duration of certain behaviors, who is involved in doing what, and more subtle factors, such as dress, nonverbal clues, and the normal and abnormal actions taken by participants.

A caution: Field notes are not journal entries. A journal records the internal state of the researcher and includes personal judgments, fears, doubts, and joys. In contradistinction, a good set of field notes provides the reader with a more straightforward description of what took place. A journal might state:

The anger I felt at the stupid way this so-called leader dealt with an obviously hurting person was compounded by what I just saw.

A field note entry about the same incident might state:

Janice looked across the room at Amy and said, as the group settled into their chairs (in a flat "tone"), "I know you don't feel a part of us, Amy. Would you tell us why?"

In addition to such verbatims, field notes attempt to recapture the immediacy and the environmental "feel" of the setting. Entries, therefore, note colors, tastes, sounds, and smells.

Not everything gets taken down in field notes. The observer selectively chooses material in accordance with the problem in the practice of ministry to be addressed by the D.Min. project. It might be interesting to observe everything, but such is not practical or possible. Often the observer, having considered the field notes just taken, sets a path for the next occasion in which field notes will be taken by asking what such notes already taken can be understood to mean, by comparing/contrasting the notes with the theory of ministry under consideration, or by naming "missed" areas that seemingly need "closer attention" in the next observation.

While time-consuming and sometimes criticized as being overly subjective, field notes graphically illustrate emerging trends and generate new ideas regarding the student's initial theorizing. Field notes "work" in large measure because implications for theory only become visible as one observes and records, over time, particular practices of ministry. Field notes, therefore, aid in the historical periodization of a project; i.e., they name "how it was on a certain day, what happened next, and how it is now." Therefore, when the case study about a particular practice of ministry is being written, data generated by disciplined use of this research tool can prove to be invaluable for the author.

What follows is one section of a case study partially based on field notes taken by Lynne Schmidt as she participated in a Milwaukee conference in preparation for the writing of her D.Min. paper, "Feminist Liturgies: Efforts Toward Creative Transformation in the Roman Catholic Church."[1] Note that Schmidt stands firmly within the pro-active stance of research methodology #3 as described in chapter four and that she presents her material in a case study format.

Womenbonding Liturgy

by Lynn Schmidt

The "Womenbonding" conference held in Milwaukee in 1982 provides an example of participation with multiple presiders. The room was arranged so that people were seated at tables in groups of seven or eight with an open space in one area created as the group focal point. The liturgy had four parts:

I. The Gathering Rite
II. The Gospel Rite
III. Breaking Bread, Sharing the Cup
IV. The Commissioning Rite

Each of these rites had a facilitator in the central area and two facilitators at each table. The liturgical action flowed back and forth between these two areas.

In *The Gathering Rite* the central facilitator welcomed those assembled and invited all to share in the celebration of the lives of common women. She led the readers and communal responses. She invited the whole group to spontaneously name groups of women oppressed in the world today.

The Gospel Rite was a danced magnificat in the central space. Each women was asked to reflect on her call and response as God's daughter.

In *The Breaking of Bread, Sharing the Cup Rite*, two facilitators from each table brought the bread and wine to the central space. As each came forward to form a semi-circle, she named herself or her affiliation: "I am Judy. I offer this bread (or share this cup) in the name of all the raped women, victims of male violence in our society." When all the tables had been represented, the central facilitator for this third rite led a prayer of praise and thanksgiving for God's actions in the world. The community responded by saying THIS IS OUR BREAD, OUR LIVES; THIS IS THE CUP WE SHARE. The leaders at the tables passed the bread and the cup. They invited the participants to name persons whom they wanted to remember in this action. As a closing response to the rite, the musicians led the group in singing Cris Williamson's "Sister."

In *The Commissioning Rite* a central facilitator challenged the congregation to live this Eucharist and to go forth to their homes and other workplaces proclaiming God's call to liberation. As a response to the commissioning homily, the dancer wove from table to table, gathering the participants in a spiral dance. She led everyone to the central space as the concluding movement of the liturgy.

*   *   *

Such field note-taking as Schmidt has done requires discipline, and the greater the time lapse between the observation and the actual writing down of the observation, the greater the loss of usable data. This means setting aside time to take notes (or to "recall") in close proximity to the event being observed. Note-taking must be understood as requiring an absolute commitment, no matter how tired the researcher. The researcher must, with discipline, bend to the task of applying pen to paper.

In summary, field notes have the following characteristics:

Pro	*Con*
Simple, low-tech, first-hand way to generate data....	A time lapse often occurs between an event and the written note....
Provides a continuous historic record of what took place....	Requires discipline on the part of the researcher to write and review the notes....
Generates issues or themes with theoretical implications....	May overemphasize the subjective side and become more of a personal journal....
Once written, can be used for retrospective critical reflection at any time.	Generates an immense amount of data, occasionally overwhelming the researcher.

2. Audio/Videotapes and the Verbatim as Ways to Generate Data from the Setting

It is hard to miss camcorders or portable tape players in today's culture. Persons applying for D.Min. in Preaching programs are instructed to provide both audiotapes and videotapes of the Sunday morning service, including the sermon. Other ministries also use this technology. Telling clients that the reflective use of verbatims with a supervisor assures a better quality of practice, many pastoral counselors regularly tape their sessions. While such sessions may, in fact, last forty-five minutes or more, a verbatim drawn from that time-frame for use in supervision (or in a case study) may cover only four or five minutes of a specific conversation. Nevertheless, pastoral counselors, secure in the understanding that such verbatims provide snapshots of the larger picture, normatively write professional reflective papers featuring verbatims drawn from such technologies.

In effect, most persons experiencing training in the human sciences regularly engage in supervisory sessions anchored by the use of such tapes. Critical reflection on the particulars of a taped and/or transcribed verbatim often is facilitated by a particular rating scale; i.e., a three- to five-point (Likert-style) continuum where, for example, an "excellent" response might garner a ranking of "one," a mediocre response rates a "three," and a destructive response is equated with a "five." Because a therapist's audiotape or videotape records the actual practice of ministry, counselors or therapists submitting their verbatims to such close scrutiny have, in addition, ethical issues connected to tape usage like confidentiality (often achieved by "masking" client identity).

The following example is drawn from several hours of transcribed tapes but reduced, in the final D. Min. paper, to a masked verbatim. It is one of many from James O'Connell's paper "Gestalt Approaches in Spiritual Direction."[2]

Spiritual Direction Application of Fantasy Dialogue

by James O'Connell

Directee:	I never find any peace. Always suffering. I often wonder why God allows so much suffering. I don't know why He makes me suffer so much.
Director:	You sound as if you would like to ask God a few questions.
Directee:	I suppose that I would like to, but I don't seem to be able to do that any more.
Director:	I would like you to try to dialogue with God now. It might feel strange, but we'll see how it goes. I want you to try to imagine what God has to say to you when you are suffering. Can you fantasize about this? First tell God about your suffering and then imagine what God's answer is. Do you want to try this?
Directee:	O.K., I'll try it. You want me to begin by telling God about myself. Is that it?

*   *   *

By structuring a D.Min. paper around several such verbatims, a D.Min. author (like O'Connell) clearly displays several candid "snapshots" of what took place within specific moments in a practice of ministry, in this case, the "practice" of spiritual direction. O'Connell's verbatim, warts and all, is presented as what such ministry "looks" like. His critical reflections assess this set of verbatims from a particular theoretical point of view.

In summary, audio/videotapes and the verbatims drawn from them have the following characteristics:

Pro	Con
Provides immediate entry to the practice of ministry and has the element of "this is really what did take place"....	Raises issues of confidentiality....
Provides useful and ample material....	Collects too much material; i.e., editing or selecting "verbatims" must take place....
Has almost become a normative technology-- equipment is usually available....	Transcription of audiotapes or editing of video is costly and requires some expertise....
Can do the same things field notes do regarding historic evolution and emerging theme development.	An unobtrusive operator is needed to "run" the video recorder; but, on occasion, even an audio recorder can be seen as obtrusive by those who are being recorded.

3. "Found" Documents as a Tool for Generating Data from the Setting

A "document" can be the written minutes of a committee, a printed sermon, a newspaper clipping, a presented paper, or the financial records of a congregation. "Documents" can also be items of clothing, the pictures on display in the narthex, the banners hanging in the sanctuary, and the cooking utensils in the church's kitchen. In that such items are "found" and are not intentionally developed by the researcher, such documents are often felt to be *unobtrusive* measures of what actually has taken place in a given setting.

One clear example of the use of such unobtrusive "found" documents in D.Min. research is represented here by the critical reflection on two of eight plates drawn by a client working with therapist C. Michael Smith. Smith relates that these drawings were what his client did to "catch" the kinds of images that filled his mind. Initially they were done without Smith's knowledge. When these drawings were discovered in a therapy session by Smith, he began to focus the therapy session around the drawings and to encourage their production. Smith's D.Min. paper, "The Pastoral Psychotherapy of Psychosis: The Active Use of Religious Resources in a Parish Context,"[3] presents a case study of Jungian pastoral psychotherapy with a man (S.K.) who is undergoing a brief psychotic reaction within a concurrent spiritual crisis:

Plate #1

by C. Michael Smith

Now I turn to the analysis of the visions and dreams, for the sessions in which we worked with these images were powerful in their efficacy upon S.K., and resulted in a continuing expansion of his ego-consciousness. . . . [Plate #1 is included in Smith's text at this point.]

The first two drawings (plate #1) attempted to depict the initial revelatory experience. At first, he said, there appeared a serpent-like rod, which glowed like "lightning." Then it changed its shape into something like the letter "E," as if it were lying on its side. It glowed in the darkness, too. It was during this visual experience that the voice began to call S.K. by name, but it did not yet tell him what it wanted. On another occasion the serpent-like light turned into a fireball and called out to him, it took the shape of a red tornado in the midst of a dark ominous cloud which wrapped around it (plate #2). The voice of God (or the devil?) began to speak, and paid him several visits from the tornado like a fireball.

* * *

Again, the drawings (plates #1-8) are documents discovered in therapy by Smith. Amazed at the rich resource they represented for work with S.K., Smith eventually would use them as the center of his D.Min. paper.

Documents used to identify data from the settings of most D.Min. projects, however, are more often drawn from the "found" historic and/or official statements of a tradition, for example the pastoral letters emerging from the offices of the Roman Catholic Church. Amy Therese Kenealy demonstrates how such documents can be used to strengthen the D.Min. paper in her case study "Nurturing Lay Pastoral Care Ministers in the Roman Catholic Parish."[4] Note how she sets the context and then utilizes the public documents of the Roman Catholic Church to frame her issue.

Theoretical Foundations of the Problem

by Amy Therese Kenealy

The mandate certificate from the Archdiocese of Chicago given to the lay pastoral care ministers reads in part:

(You) are appointed an auxiliary minister of holy communion to the sick in the Archdiocese of Chicago. This ministry is entrusted in accordance with *The Apostolic Constitution: The Sacrament of Anointing and the Pastoral Care of the Sick,* of November 30, 1972.

Although initially conceived by many in the Church to be a limited ministry of bringing communion to the sick, the second part of the mandate points to a larger mission:

You are to be a sign of support and concern this church has for the sick and elderly. Visit them, share with them the word of God in scripture, pray with them for the Church and the world. When they cannot gather with us on Sunday, bring to them the body and blood of the Lord and so make us one in communion.

It is because of this larger mission that lay pastoral care ministers need to be nurtured in order to be more effective in their ministry.

Joseph Cardinal Bernadin, in his pastoral letter *In Service to One Another* (1985), states that laity who serve in church ministries must be enabled, enriched, supported, coordinated and trained. This places serious responsibility on the pastor of a local parish to provide for the nurturing of the lay pastoral care minister.

*   *   *

Kenealy's work with these documents of her religious tradition grounds certain expectations for her case study of lay ministers within her Roman Catholic parish. Because *tradition* is highly valued by the Archdiocese of Chicago (her "audience"), such documents as Kenealy includes in her case study bear weight for her evaluative comments that will follow.

Once such documents have been located, the D.Min. student must engage in "documentary analysis." Documentary analysis is a systematic procedure by which the meaning of the document is "unpacked." One way to do this is to set the document's content more firmly within the historic context in which the document occurred. In Kenealy's paper, for example, it helps to know that the "Certificate from the Archdiocese of Chicago" and the "Pastoral Letter of Joseph Cardinal Bernadin" are in the public realm. No one questions their authenticity. A more complex question has to do with how such documents can be interpreted. Judgments must be made regarding what can be claimed on the basis of particular documents. Too much occasionally gets claimed, and sometimes an over-reliance upon a particular document skews an interpretation. In the example of Kenealy's presented documents, one must also ask "What do these data mean?" and "Are they relevant to the case under study?" In addition, such documents cannot be evaluated outside their own time-frame; i.e., if the document is from a previous century, it is unrealistic to argue with the document's lack of some modern understanding or theme.

Documents, despite these concerns, are often used to challenge or to complement those themes that seem to be emerging from interviews, field observations, and other research tools. Such inclusion of data from documents can be interwoven within the narrative flow, adding a contextual richness and complexity to the case study. When the historic context of a document is certain, there is a certain unavoidability to the data presented in the case.

In summary, documents have the following characteristics:

Pro	Con
Documents are unavoidable presentations from the historic past....	It is hard to always determine what weight to assign a particular document....
A document is one fairly simple way to discover what a specific group or representatives felt about specific issues....	One can inappropriately read back into a document contemporary themes or lack thereof....
Documents provide a richness to any contextual assessment of a particular moment in time.	Sometimes documents are hard to locate; once located many have confidentiality issues connected to them.

Summary

Collecting data from *the setting* of the D.Min. project can involve the use of one or more tools like field notes, audio/ videotapes, and "found" documents. Field notes are observations written down by the D.Min. student in close proximity to the setting. Field notes can chronicle the historic progression of a ministry project as well as document what the setting currently looks like. Not everything gets written down; field notes produce stronger data as the researcher becomes more precise regarding what is being observed.

Audio/videotapes are tools used to capture an actual occasion, enabling a team or an evaluative researcher to replay what took place. While the transcribed audio verbatim and the edited video tape promote a variety of research approaches, the researcher is always faced with ethical decisions related to confidentiality. In any case, an unedited tape, whether audio or video, should not be allowed to "sit" on the researcher's desk; some technical ability (typing verbatims; editing videotapes, etc.) must be employed.

"Found" documents are historic in nature--they are "in" the setting, and they provide an unobtrusive way to gather data. For example, as historians count and map the debris of the Battle of Gettysburg, each musketball or worn button is understood as a historical document. D. Min. researchers also have similar documents within a project's setting--banners, music scores, governing board minutes, the preacher's robe. Simply naming the presence of a certain document is not enough; the document must be analyzed. "Documentary analyses" are a systematic way to discover the multiple meanings contained within documents. A researcher must note the interpretive lens brought to such a process, but documents add a certain authenticity (and any interpretive lens can be questioned by a reader).

These three tools--field notes, audio and video tapes, and "found" documents--are useful in collecting data from the *setting* of a given D.Min. project.

Notes to Chapter Six

1. Lynne Schmidt, "Feminist Liturgies: Efforts Toward Creative Transformation in the Roman Catholic Church," in *Spiritual Nurture and Congregational Development*, ed. Perry LeFevre and W. Widick Schroeder (Chicago: Exploration Press, 1984).

2. James O'Connell, "Gestalt Approaches in Spiritual Direction," in *Spiritual Nurture and Congregational Development*, ed. Perry LeFevre and W. Widick Schroeder (Chicago: Exploration Press, 1984).

3. C. Michael Smith, "The Pastoral Psychotherapy of Psychosis: The Active Use of Religious Resources in a Parish Context," in *Creative Ministries in Contemporary Christianity*, ed. Perry LeFevre and W. Widick Schroeder (Chicago: Exploration Press, 1991),

4. Amy Therese Kenealy, "Nurturing Lay Pastoral Care Ministers in the Roman Catholic Parish," in *Creative Ministries in Contemporary Christianity*, ed. Perry LeFevre and W. Widick Schroeder (Chicago: Exploration Press, 1991),

CHAPTER SEVEN

GENERATING DATA FROM THE PARTICIPANTS

The D.Min. student also faces the task of collecting data from *participants* within the ministry setting. Such collection of data often takes shape by (1) holding personal or group interviews, (2) engaging individuals or groups with paper and pencil questionnaires, or (3) by requesting the confidential sharing of participant's assigned personal journals, diaries, art work, or written "homework." Again, as was noted in chapter six, many of these activities are ones with which the professional minister is quite familiar.

1. Interviews as an Initial Way to Gather Data from Participants

Who should be interviewed? In part, the answer to this question depends upon both the number of potential interviewees and the purpose of the interview. If the D.Min. student is working with a group of eight to twelve people, that student probably ought to interview everyone. But, if the student has three hundred persons in the ministry setting, that student either needs to interview a true random sample (in which everyone has the same chance of being chosen) or *purposively choose* and interview a representative number of persons. How many persons should be purposively chosen to be representative in part is answered by the particulars of a given project, but six in-depth interviews conceivably could generate more than 250 transcribed typewritten pages and initially take anywhere from five to twelve hours to complete. Perhaps this much data collection is more than what is needed.

PURPOSIVE SAMPLE. What goes into the "purposive choice" of certain persons to be interviewed is determined by the nature of what is being explored. A purposive sample, therefore, is done for certain named reasons. For example, persons are purposively chosen who may be (1) aware, (2) "typical" of the group, (3) politically savvy, or (4) generally knowledgeable. Persons also might be interviewed because (1) they fit certain demographics,

(2) they were chosen by someone else, (3) they have a reputation, or (4) they represent those "in" and "out," or "for" or "against." Purposive samples often are based on convenience; i.e., "these are the folk I could interview, given where I was located."

An example might indicate some of the subtle issues connected with such "purposive" samples. A D.Min. student wished to critically evaluate a religious education program housed in a particular congregation. The host pastor made a positive response to her query regarding the project, but indicated a select list of folk that "should be interviewed." Accepting this task as her entry require-ment, the D.Min. student interviewed both the nominated persons and then, at a later time, interviewed a second group she intentionally identified on her own after two weeks observation of the program. In effect, there were two "purposive samples," and while the data generated from both sets of interviews were considerable, she felt that the initial interview list was politically "sus-pect." Indeed, her list generated data from certain persons who were intention-ally "missed" by those in charge of the program. All such "purposive samples," as these examples demonstrate, ought to be clearly named or described in a D.Min. case study. However, once a sample is chosen, interviews occur with individuals or with focus groups in three ways: forced-option, open-ended, and unstructured.

Forced-option interviews are structured around a set format in which "yes" and "no" are perfectly acceptable responses. These interview schedules are often built upon Likert-type options. For example:

Example of Forced-Option Interview Format

Date_____ Name of Interviewee_____

Setting_____ Position_____

Topic_____

A. To what extent are you involved in the youth ministry of First Church, Middletown?

* Youth Fellowship	1	2	3
* Youth Choir	1	2	3
* Youth Saturday Service Club	1	2	3
* Youth Basketball League	1	2	3
* Youth Chaplains	1	2	3

1 = not at all; 2 = to a certain extent; 3 = a great deal.

*   *   *

Either the Likert style or a similar logically exhaustive instrument is used in order to cover every option. This format is often used in phone/market survey or poll research, and is carefully field-tested in advance of use in order to eliminate any bugs or poorly-worded items. Such "interviews" are often short in duration precisely because of the high volume of interviews that are scheduled to occur.

Open-ended interviews are built around areas (or "items") that are believed to be critical to the practice of ministry under consideration. These items, generated by the researcher's theory or by data from some other instrument, set the framework for the interview, and every person is interviewed using that same set of items. If a given interview includes, for example, open-ended items on (1) culture, (2) spirituality, (3) individualism, and (4) community, then every interviewee will be asked to reflect upon the same questions.

In the following example, Anne Abernethy composed a D.Min. interview schedule that is primarily open-ended. Her D.Min. paper was entitled "When the Minister Has a Baby."[1]

Interviews

by Anne B. Abernethy

Through a process of referral from acquaintances and denominational officials, I made direct contact with twenty-four clergywomen and one spouse of a clergywoman. With eighteen of these persons I conducted personal interviews. . . .

The primary criteria for choosing persons to interview were that they either be pregnant or already have children and that the pregnancy coincide with service to a church (or in two cases, service in a ministry-related field). All respondents were asked questions which highlighted the following areas: practical considerations (e.g., plans for maternity leave, announcing the news to the congregation), intrapersonal issues (e.g., self-identity concerns, feelings about the impending birth), and spiritual issues (e.g., change in theological/world view). . . .

* * *

For the purpose of this book, Abernethy's open-ended interview schedule is moved from her appendix to this more central position:

INTERVIEW SCHEDULE

    I.   *Identifying Information*
          name
          age

race
address
marital status
denomination
current job position
names and ages of children
spouse's occupation (now)
spouse's occupation
  (at time of child[ren]'s birth)
year of ordination or other set-apart status
  (indicate your status)

1. Describe yourself (age, job position, etc.) and the situation in which you worked (type of community, size of church, etc.) when you were expecting your child(ren).
2. Did you choose to resign your ministerial position as a result of your pregnancy? If so, at what point and for how long?

II. *Practical Considerations*

3. How did you announce the news of the impending birth to your congregation?
4. Describe any changes in your working schedule that resulted from the increased demands of pregnancy.
5. What plans, if any, did you make for taking time off prior to and/or after the child's birth?
6. What support, if any, did you receive from your congregation and your denomination concerning job-related issues which arose as a result of your pregnancy (i.e., leave of absence, modification of working schedule, etc.)?

III. *Intrapersonal Issues*

7. How did your understanding of yourself (as a woman and as a professional) change as a result of pregnancy and childbirth? What identity issues were raised for you?
8. Describe any changes in your model of ministry (leadership style, preaching style, interaction with church members, etc.) that resulted from the experience of having a child.
9. Were you aware of any anger that surfaced for you in response to members of your family and/or congregation? What pregnancy and/or post-partum issues precipitated your anger? How did the working through of this anger affect your ministry--both positively and negatively?

IV. *Interpersonal Issues*

10. Comment on any changes in behavior/ attitude of congregational members toward you that occurred as a result of your pregnancy.

11. Concerning your pregnancy, was there any significant differ-ence in response from male church members as compared with female church members? In particular, how did the women of the church react to you as a woman combining a professional role with the role of mother?

12. As a result of your pregnancy, were you discouraged (openly or subtly) from performing certain functions within the church? If so, please describe.

13. Describe any new avenues of ministry which opened to you as a result of your pregnancy.

14. How did the congregation's reaction to your pregnancy com-pare with their reaction to you after the baby was born?

V. *Spiritual Issues*

15. What spiritual issues were raised for you as a result of preg-nancy and childbirth? What changes occurred in your theolo-gy/ world-view?

16. Describe any changes that occurred in the content of your sermons and in your reflections on such pastoral functions as marriages and funerals.

17. What new awareness did your congregation gain as a result of your pregnancy and the birth of your child?

VI. *The Experience in Toto*

18. Overall, how would you describe the experience of being pregnant while actively engaged in ministry?

19. How did it feel to share the experience of pregnancy and par-enting with the people of your congregation? Were you able to allow them to be supportive? Did you ever resent the lack of privacy afforded you as you shared the experience?

20. If you have had more than one child, comment on your adap-tation to pregnancy (as related to your ministry) for subse-quent children as compared with the first experience.

VII. *Other Issues*

21. Did you breast-feed your baby? If so, what issues were raised for you and your congregation as a result of this?

22. What was the experience like for your husband? How did he help to plan for the baby and then later participate in child care? What was the congregation's reaction to him as an expectant and actual father?

23. If you have lost children through a miscarriage, stillbirth, etc., what issues were raised for you as related to your min-istry?

24. Would you be interested in participating in a workshop designed to explore the issues discussed here? If so, what questions and/or other issues would you like to raise as related to this topic?

* * *

Unstructured Interviews, our third category, have the flavor of in-depth conversations. If there is a "key informant" within the ministry project (a person whose insights are valued by the D.Min. student), then while no formal instrument is used, every meeting or conversation with such a person is perceived by the D.Min. researcher to be an unstructured interview.

Example of An Unstructured Interview Transcript

Page #

Tape T, Date
Calvin, a 16-year-old in Church X. Our third interview.
Setting: At 6 p.m. in the basement of church.
Interviewer (hereafter W.M.): Well, I'm glad you were able to get the bus. I know it's tough for you to be here, but I need to know what you think the purpose is for the youth group at church. Let's jump in there.
Interviewee (hereafter C.): My sense is that it's to give us something to do....

* * *

The D.Min. student who does an unstructured interview on Saturday ought to replay it several times the following week in order to sense what was said that may have been missed at the time of the interview. Such an initial listening may result in a "follow-up" interview. ("Calvin, as I ran through the tape of our conversation last Saturday, you said something I don't understand. Could you clarify it for me?")

In every interview, whether forced-option, open-ended, or unstructured, how the interviewer "names" the situation to the interviewee is critical to the outcome of the interview. For example, if the interviewer does not provide confidentiality ("no real names will be used in my paper; situations will be masked; you can have the tape cassette after I have it transcribed; you can read the paper before I put it into a public library"), the interviewee may deliberately mislead the conversation or present inaccurate information. In any interview, the interviewee should be guaranteed confidentiality and be encouraged to talk freely, but the interviewer should always "listen" to more than the verbal content. Nervous laughter, pauses, grimaces, body language, etc. should be described and included on the tape transcript of the interview. Since data excerpted from interviews will eventually become visible in a public document (the published D.Min. end paper), however, confidentiality to those being interviewed should be the bottom line.

The actual interview can be (1) audiotaped, (2) videotaped, (3) note-taken during the interview, or (4) re-called in written form as close to the interview as possible. The audiotape can always be accessed, but given that format, some thought ought to go into where the interview will occur, if there is a power supply (cord/battery), and whether or not the tape-recorder is adequate to the task. While audiotapes can be re-played in a very "raw" form and never be transcribed (that is, become a typed hard copy), my preference is for a fully typed transcript or one that has, in addition, been edited. Persons who can use a word processor have a definite advantage in sorting such data. (More about this in chapter nine.) In any case, wide transcript margins should be kept for notes.

In summary, interviews have the following characteristics:

Pro	Con
The direct connection of the interviewer/interviewee encourages depthful exploration....	The interviewee may seek to "please" the one doing the interview....
A single, solid interview can quickly expand the vision of the interviewer.	Labor, time, and resource intensive.

2. Questionnaires as a Way to Gather Data from Participants

Questionnaires are paper and pencil instruments designed to collect particular bits of information from participants within ministry settings. On balance, when a reasonable return rate is assured, questionnaires are a quick and simple way to obtain a fairly solid reading from a setting. Some D.Min. students have reported that they assured a high rate of return when they picked a good occasion to use the instrument (committee meeting, program), and when they personally collected the completed questionnaires. Others have utilized the questionnaire as a Sunday morning worship bulletin insert. Still others have only used such instruments with purposively chosen focus groups, often in tandem with individual or group interviews. Regardless of how it will be used, the

questionnaire ought to be pre-tested with a congenial group in order to eliminate or re-word poorly constructed questions. Once this is done, the questionnaire provides a quick quantitative assessment. (Anne Abernethy, in the interview schedule listed above, used essentially the same schedule as a questionnaire for some persons who were too far removed for her to interview.)

In practice, the questionnaire usually is kept relatively simple for D.Min.
projects. For example, one D.Min. in Preaching project asked identified
respondents who agreed to listen to four sermons to complete the following
questionnaire after each sermon:

Questionnaire

by Richard Kirchherr
(used by permission)

Sermon Title:_____

Biblical Passage:_____

(1) As closely as you are able, recreate the Biblical passage on which the
sermon was based.

(2) Does this passage have any relevance in your life? Why or why not?
(If a specific experience is relevant, please share it.)

(3) Was this style of preaching engaging for you? Why or why not?

*   *   *

Based on the information gathered from this simple three-item questionnaire, the D.Min. student then was able to frame a more depthful group interview. Without claiming too much, Kirchherr therefore was able to utilize
material gathered from this simple two-step process to aid him in his case study.

A more complex questionnaire is contained in Dale Schumm's "The
Belmont Model: An Experiment in Congregational Renewal."[2] Schumm uses
Likert-style continuums of 5 for much, to 1 for little, so that the persons
involved in the renewal process could rate how much they felt they were a part
of it, how clearly they felt heard, and how well they sensed that the process was
related to their own theological understanding of the church. The following
example from that paper gives results for the various choices as percentages of
the total number responding:

Belmont Model
Questionnaire #11

by Dale Schumm

Item #2. How clearly do you think your opinions were heard? Please circle one: 1 2 3 4 5.
1 = not at all; 2 = on occasion; 3 = more than occasionally; 4 = frequently; 5 = on every occasion.

[Schumm notes his result in percentages. This item had the following response: 1 = zero percent; 2 = seven percent; 3 = seven percent; 4 = forty-two percent; 5 = forty-four percent; total = one hundred percent.]

* * *

Again, caution is used in making too strong an interpretation regarding data gathered from such a questionnaire. Shumm states: "From the results [of the complete questionnaire] it would appear that those who participated felt a strong sense of being a part of the entire process." Nowhere does he make any unwarranted claims regarding this simple instrument.

Schumm's use of the Likert-style five-point continuum is a popular way to structure the questionnaire, but the questionnaire also can be used to collect other statistical information through the use of a variety of formats:

Example of Mixed Questionnaire

1. Your name is _____.
2. The number of years you have been a member of this group is
   a. Zero to five _____
   b. Six to ten _____
   c. Eleven to twenty _____
   d. Twenty-one or more _____
3. The time set aside for prayer on the retreat was
   a. too much _____
   b. about right _____
   c. not enough _____
4. How would you evaluate the leadership team's role on this retreat? Check one:

_____	_____	_____	_____	_____
Very Good	Good	Average	Poor	Very Poor

* * *

While this example shows how a mixed questionnaire may be used, questionnaires also can provide opportunities for the respondent's open-ended comments. For example, note how alternatives "c" and "d" in the following questionnaire are followed by an "open-ended" question:

Example of Closed and Open-Ended Questionnaire

5. Was this retreat helpful as an event to explore the spiritual dimensions of faith?
   a. _____ Yes, to a great extent.
   b. _____ Yes, somewhat.
   c. _____ No, not as much as I had hoped.
   d. _____ Probably detrimental.
If "c" or "d," what would you like to see happen to improve future events?

*   *   *

Open-ended questions (like the one following "d" in the above example) are often used to elicit extended and more thoughtful responses from respondents.

Questionnaires can occur, whatever their specific form, with either individuals or with focus groups (smaller gatherings of six to ten persons purposively chosen for the questionnaire process). Dale H. Schumm's D.Min. paper (mentioned above) utilized what he calls the "natural cluster groupings" in his congregation for just such a focused group questionnaire process. He reports the responses he collected from the use of open-ended questions.

The Cluster Questionnaire

by Dale Schumm

Recently, the cluster members were asked to finish open-ended statements. Each of these statements elicited responses such as the following:
1. My personal goals for my cluster are _____.
   - to learn to share myself with others in depth.
   - to support each other and to win new members to the church.
   - to study the Bible and current issues.
   - to integrate fun, fellowship, and worship.
2. What I want most from my cluster is _____.
   - to be a link with the larger church.
   - to be a testing ground for ideas.
   - to be an enlargement of my family.
   - acceptance, love, support, and caring.
   - to help to develop my Christian life.

- Christ-centered fellowship, help in time of need.
- affirmation and discipline, a strong support group.
- help in discerning my lifestyle and Christian walk.
These responses indicate that clusters are meeting a significant need in the lives of their members.

*   *   *

Again, note both Schumm's use of a written, open-ended questionnaire within a focus group and the claims he has made on the basis of data gathered from this instrument ("these responses indicate that clusters are meeting a significant need in the lives of members"). Schumm is careful not to claim more than the tool warrants, but he does share enough of his data so that we can make our own assessment.

Questionnaires can be complex, but for the D.Min. process, the simpler the questionnaire, the more likelihood of useable data and a high rate of return. Questionnaires can be used to collect basic demographic data, data concentrated around "themes," or targeted data in response to specific questions. Closed, Likert-type continuums, and open-ended formats are frequently used in D.Min. questionnaires. Questionnaires should be checked for problems in advance of their actual usage. Invite three or four thoughtful folk to complete the instrument. Such "field-testing" often surfaces poorly worded sentences and badly worded or loaded questions.

In summary, questionnaires have the following characteristics:

Pro	Con
Questionnaires are quick, simple, and effective ways to collect a considerable amount of data....	Questionnaires only skim the surface....
They provide a clear glimpse of groups and individuals....	They are notorious for low return rates....
They can be designed to fit very specific needs in D.Min. projects....	When too long or too complicated, people rush to completion....
They often surface themes and issues the researcher might overlook.	On occasion, persons unsure of where they stand or interested in not sounding too "radical," seek the middle.

3. Assigned Homework as a Way to Gather Data from Participants

In addition to questionnaires and interviews, D.Min. students often collect participant data by assigning, suggesting, or requesting artwork, diaries, personal journals, or other similar forms of written or drawn "homework." Such homework, used with confidentiality, can also anchor D.Min. papers.

In a D.Min. paper entitled "A Therapist's View of Spiritual Direction: A Case Study," Thomas M. Holden, S.J. presents data from the participant's side of spiritual direction by directly sharing from that person's journal.³ In this instance, the person's journal was an agreed "assignment." It was not, therefore, a "found" document. Holden shares some of that material with the readers of his case study.

Mary's Journal

by Thomas J. Holden, S.J.

After working with Mary for over a year, she began to deal with the more basic issues lying underneath all her struggles. This became clear to her when she was writing her journal. I would like to let her express it in her own words. The following quote is a rather lengthy one, but it portrays the essence of her conflict. She highlighted her references to herself by circling the personal pronouns in red. This, then, is what she wrote:

Yesterday, Tom asked me, "What is the struggle?" I couldn't answer that then. After talking about how I feel about having to give up my role on the liturgy team, the Lord confronted me with myself.

The struggle (life-long) is with me--my inordinate concern with me. That's why I feel burned out--I wasn't doing those things more for the Lord than for myself. Of course, this wasn't conscious.

I hate me. God, damn you, why have you let me be this way for so many years? I hate you--God--why have I been this way? I can't love, never could. I want to end it all. Damn you, for allowing me to be so stupid, ignorant, selfish-narrow all this time. Damn. I am trapped by me. . . [Mary's Journal continues].

*   *   *

Written or assigned homework (like Mary's journal) can be useful as a spiritual director like Holden critically reflects in a D.Min. paper on his practice of ministry. But religious educators, for example, can also assign and collect similar examples of classroom, retreat, or camping educational homework. While such homework often can be included as an added-on research tool, a participant's diary of a thirteen-day canoe trip can provide the core of a D.Min. project, as could the art work resting on the children's easel in the nursery room of the local church. Imagination is required for the appropriate inclusion and design of such assigned "homework," but it would seem apparent that while D.Min. papers are primarily word-oriented, this particular research tool can be used to access not only words, but other forms of communication as well.

For example, one D.Min. researcher, deep into a youth ministry project, introduced the use of newsprint and magic markers as a complementary part of an oral interview process. At one point in every interview he invited the interviewee to sketch (in whatever way the interviewee desired) what the youth ministry program at this particular church "looked like, or was all about." Those sketches provided some convincing images that were later used by him in a paper on "effective models of youth ministry." He would claim the sketches spoke "louder than words."

Yet another D.Min. researcher, utilizing photographs of four symbols located within the congregation she was studying, asked a purposively chosen group of people to choose one from the four and to write a personal essay on what that symbol meant. By doing so, she quickly discovered the core elements of what formed the "identity" of the congregation.

Specific tasks such as these are often intuitively assigned by the D.Min. student out of circumstances that have emerged from the ministry context. In one sense, the "pro-active" research method affirms this tool because it assumes a co-researcher stance; i.e., *together* certain "assignments" are agreed upon, and when completed, can be said to express deep-felt understandings.

In summary, assigned homework has the following characteristics:

Pro	Con
Assigned homework can pinpoint certain hard-to-get-at issues....	Much of this is an intuitive, "felt" response; it may not be generalizable....
It also connects with those who wish to "dive deeply"....	Sometimes these images are difficult to convey; D.Min. papers are word-oriented....
It can also engage senses beyond the printed page.	It sometimes appears as idiosyncratic musings, ultimately unconnected.

Summary

Interviews, questionnaires, and assigned homework provide data from the point-of-view of participants. (1) For interviews, the critical issue is who gets chosen and why. The D.Min. student usually interviews a "purposively chosen" sample rather than a "random sample," and assures complete confidentiality. The student also plans, well in advance of the interviewing moment, for the technical aspects of the interview. Whether closed, open-ended, or unstructed, interviews produce large amounts of raw data for which ongoing analysis is greatly encouraged. (2) Written questionnaires access more persons in a shorter period of time, but the instrument itself must be carefully structured and does not provide the depth of the interview. (3) D. Min. researchers may also ask participants for assigned homework. Such homework may be instantly helpful or highly idiosyncratic, but often is counted upon to provide access to the intuitive side of persons in ministry.

The appropriate selection and the use of specific participant-oriented tools are critical concerns for the D.Min. student. The goal, after all, is to choose a tool and use it in ways that are both appropriate to the ministry being observed and pragmatically useful in the collection of data. No one tool can "do it all." Several tools may, in tandem, provide just the right amount of evaluative power.

Notes to Chapter Seven

1. Anne B. Abernethy, "When the Minister Has a Baby," in *Creative Ministries in Contemporary Christianity*, ed. Perry LeFevre and W. Widick Schroeder (Chicago: Exploration Press, 1991).
2. Dale Schumm, "The Belmont Model: An Experiment in Congregational Renewal," in *Spiritual Nurture and Congregational Development*, ed. Perry LeFevre and W. Widick Schroeder (Chicago: Exploration Press, 1984).
3. Thomas M. Holden, S.J., "A Therapist's View of Spiritual Direction: A Case Study," in *Spiritual Nurture and Congregational Development*, ed. Perry LeFevre and W. Widick Schroeder (Chicago: Exploration Press, 1984).

CHAPTER EIGHT

GENERATING DATA FROM THE RESEARCHER

While some research methodologies deny the importance of data generated by the researcher's own internal (and highly subjective) dialogue, the D.Min. process accents such data as necessary and important information. Data generated by the subjective valuing process of the researcher is therefore considered to be of great value in building a case study. This is a major philosophical leap. It would seem, however, that for ministerial transformation in the D.Min. process, such data (and the critical reflection generated by focusing on such data) is absolutely central to the task. Of primary importance to this chapter, therefore, is that the Doctor of Ministry student who uses a case study methodology must be encouraged to access their internal state as one of the "domains" that can be tapped into for valuable data. (Two other domains beyond that of the *researcher* are the *setting*, discussed in chapter six, and the *participants* in the setting, discussed in chapter seven.)

The primary way such data gets accessed (written down) by the researcher is through the discipline of a personal journal. A journal, however, is not the same as a diary. A diary often is built upon free association; in contradistinction, a D.Min. journal is designed to access the internal dialogue of the D.Min. student who is dealing with the particulars (and therefore focused upon) a specific D.Min. project. Dated journal entries, therefore, are occasions for the exploration of D.Min.-related emotional concerns, sudden insights, and epiphanies. By indicating through the project proposal "how" and "when" such entries will occur, the journal becomes a disciplined way that data gets collected from the "self."

Since the keeping of a journal connects its author to an ongoing reflection process that often is composed of "ups" and "downs," central to the use of a journal is a personal willingness to be transformed by those whose lives have become a part of the once distant "researcher." For example, Maria C. Gabriel details her transformation as she engaged in the ministry of Genesis House, a new "home for prostitutes." Gabriel's story is called "Genesis House: Journeys of Transformation."[1] Listen to her journal entry following one encounter:

The pain, anger and shame that accompanies this process of transformation is still with me. I am constantly being challenged. One of the women, after talking to me for a while, told me how she knew that people did not want to come near her, because she wasn't clean. Then she turned to me and asked, "Are you afraid of me?" I was taken aback by the directness of this question and was touched deeply. After a moment I said, "No, I am not afraid." She then asked, "Will you hold me for a while?"

* * *

Gabriel concludes: "I have had to get in touch with feelings that society deadens in me."

As this illustration suggests, when the journal becomes a regular discipline of the researcher as this person is immersed within the unfolding D.Min. project, surprising data emerges. On another occasion, a D.Min. student engaged in hospital chaplaincy and concerned about the spiritual journal of the caregiver began to recognize the importance of how her dreams now connected to her D.Min. project. As the focus of the D.Min. project was her own journey as a caregiver, the dream work she recorded within her journal became a primary source of data for her ongoing critical reflection with her supervisor.

Form: A Journal Entry

Journals can take a variety of forms and can be understood as occurring in a variety of ways, but Doctor of Ministry advisors who recommend the keeping of a journal suggest that the student engage in writing the journal in advance of, during, and after the ministry project. Such advice suggests that advisors are clear regarding the longitudinal value of data generated by this instrument; i.e., hunches, concerns, and insights occur over time, and the disciplined (and dated) use of a journal can access such change.

Example of Journal Entry

Journal entry #4, October 10th. I am at home.... I wonder if this thing will get off the ground! Two of the key people asked to see me tomorrow. I'm not certain they trust me, and I'm not certain why, but tomorrow will tell the tale, I hope....

. . . .

Journal entry #12, November 6th. I'm at the restaurant following the group's meeting. ...the one person I spoke with back in October has become a key player in this project. Today he unloaded a lot of deep secrets that have apparently blocked this community at some important junctures....

. . . .

Journal entry #22, December 12th. My office. ...I'm putting together, in a gut way, that this place has its own story. And some folk (like Jim) are "keepers of the story." They can let you in, or lock you out, simply by telling or withholding the story....

*   *   *

By comparing these and other entries, the Doctor of Ministry researcher "tracks" the emergence of certain ideas and themes. Such themes may conflict with or add to the project's initiating theory. Sometimes, as in the above example, data coalesces into what can be called an "emerging theme." In the first journal entry (see above), a "key person" was making a decision about "trusting" the D.Min. student with "community secrets." When certain things occurred, "Jim" (who held the secrets) decided to tell the story. Because of this process, the D.Min. student has a sense of how this theme seemed to be emerging, and therefore is keeping a close watch on how "telling the story" has further implications for ministry.

Confirming the Data

Some research methodologies suggest that the insights gained through the use of the more subjective research tools (like field notes, journals, and interviews) need to be "reality checked." A reality check for the written description primarily derived from field notes occurs when that description is read and critiqued by an "insider" familiar with the ministry context. In similar fashion, cases or interpretive themes emerging or built from interviews are reality-checked when a focus group of persons drawn from the ministry context is presented with and asked to react to the cases/themes. Their comments and concerns also become a part of the gathered data.

For example, as I described the congregations researched for the book *Black and White Styles of Youth Ministry: Two Congregations in America* (New York: Pilgrim Press, 1991), I submitted the emerging descriptions to insiders from the congregations, eventually incorporating their comments into my final descriptions. In similar fashion, I presented the emerging themes of that research to a one-day focus group composed of twenty black and twenty white pastors; their comments were recorded and selectively included in my final manuscript.

Summary

The D.Min. researcher values the subjective data generated within the researcher through the process of ministry. A journal often is used to "catch" this data. Entries are disciplined in form, open in style. The possibility of comparing entries in such a journal over time makes them particularly relevant to the ministerial process and also to D.Min. research. Insights resulting from such subjective data should be checked--with "insiders" or with persons familiar with the setting--and then factored into the final narrative of the case study. The resulting case study benefits from authenticity and uniqueness when such data is included. Journals have the following characteristics:

Pro	*Con*
The journal accesses the internal hunches, questions, concerns, and insights of the D.Min. student....	The journal produces subjective data and can therefore "skew" research....
It provides a simple means to generate the often intuitive warrants of the "practice of ministry"....	Without a "reality check," journaling can be dismissed as "only" subjective interpretation....
Journals are easy to do; all that is required is paper, pen, and some time.	"Good" journaling requires discipline to be useful; the use of a journal must become a regularized practice.

Notes to Chapter Eight

1. Maria C. Gabriel, "Genesis House: Journeys of Transformation," in *Creative Ministries in Contemporary Christianity*, ed. Perry LeFevre and W. Widick Schroeder (Chicago: Exploration Press, 1991).

CHAPTER NINE

CASE STUDY AS NARRATIVE: CODING AND PRESENTING THE DATA

To "code the data" means to sort through the information now made available as gathered by the D.Min. researcher through the use of various research tools, and to organize it so that it can be presented in some communicable fashion. For example, throughout this book we have seen how such "coded data" has been woven into the descriptive narrative of case studies so that readers inductively might come to agree that the author's conclusions "make sense." The D.Min. papers quoted in this manual have been chosen as competent examples because they do exactly this kind of thing; they share methodological choices and ground the arguments presented to the reader through the case study with enough data so that the reader senses the honesty and the worth of each case study.

Interactive Coding

Coding data, when begun early in the project, is an interactive process that helps the D.Min. student make important decisions about the direction of the case study. Because a case study primarily relies upon such inductive thinking, the act of coding data (looking at every piece of data with an eye to how it makes sense) "points" the researcher in the midst of a D.Min. project toward certain documents, interviews to be made, or observations that seem to be lacking. This process--working to reformulate ever clearer and sharper questions in light of what has already been observed within the project's boundaries-- "works" only when the researcher is disciplined in the interactive coding of data. If the researcher waits to sort it all out at the end of data collection, a formidable amount of material will need to be faced. Often this data simply "sits" on the researcher's desk; in order to be effective, the process of coding data must occur over time. Six interviews done over three occasions can produce as many as 300 transcribed pages. Add to this the possibility of several months of field notes plus a personal journal, and a virtual mountain of "data" emerges. What to do?

It therefore cannot be overstressed that data coding must be an ongoing process. Themes or hunches that begin to emerge in early notes need to be ongoingly pursued, eliminated, or confirmed. Eventually the researcher will become familiar enough with the data to recognize how it is beginning to coalesce into separate sets of metaphors, ideas, phrases, or themes. Such themes tend to surface because collected data often begins to display similarities; i.e., an emerging theme exhibits "internal homogeneity." All the "apples" that make up a theme come together. A second principle follows: the researcher does not put "apples" into the same bin as the one where the "oranges" are being placed. That is, there must be clear differences exhibited between "apples" and "oranges" (external heterogeneity) as the researcher moves to clarify dissimilar themes. While these two principles often result in clearly separable categories, it should also be noted that some data remains "fuzzy"; i.e., some "apples" exhibit signs of "orangeness," and vice versa. Coding data must be a process that remains open to such ambiguity.

An Example: Coding Data

The following verbatim is a fictive conversation between an interviewer and a congregant. In that the questions asked are open-ended, they tend to elicit many "bits" of data, some of which are germane to the D.Min. problem in the practice of ministry, and some of which are not. Read the verbatim, but do so with an eye toward "coding the data."

Verbatim: Coding Data

Question: Tell me about the committee.
Answer: The committee is composed of eight members. Usually it
           has its act together, but this year it has fought all year. The
           conservatives suggest it wants to eliminate some things and
           open up some things, but the old hands won't let them.
Question: Tell me what you mean when you say "some things"?

*   *   *

Data are those ordinary bits and pieces of information found within the context and, more specifically, discovered within the D.Min. project's boundaries as those boundaries have been determined by the D.Min. student. "Coding" is a way to move raw data (like this verbatim) into more usable forms.

Several pieces of data can be located in this verbatim. But first, note that we need a *locator code*. Let's say this verbatim is from an audiotape (T), that it is tape #6, and that it is taken from page 14 of the transcribed tape. A locator code, therefore, might identify something from page fourteen of this verbatim as T6-14. Now we can move the verbatim into and out of a number of interactions with other verbatims and pieces of data, but because a locator code has been determined, we can always go back to the actual source (page 14 of audiotape #6). Coded data can then be compared, contrasted, "moved around," and eventually organized into "themes." For example, in the above verbatim, a D.Min. student might recognize data that fits with other material from the project that is tied to a theme of "structure"; i.e., "the committee is composed of eight members." The researcher might want to use this line as a direct quote footnoted as "T6-14" in a section of the case study describing and analyzing the structure of the ministry being studied.

But there might also be interest in a second theme (as suggested by the use of the phrase "old hands") and also interest in a third theme (as suggested by the animosity of "old hands vs. conservatives"). A substantive theme, that may be the overriding value of this verbatim, however, might be discovered by following the meaning of a fifth theme (the phrase "to eliminate some things and open up some things"). The researcher might have other data that suggests (or does not suggest) that this phrase is the key theme of the case study.

Each of these phrases, sentences, and parts taken directly from the verbatim, therefore, presents data; for the D.Min. student the question is: "What data is relevant to my project?" An important note: the person being interviewed may skew the interview for a variety of reasons. Such attempts at skewing the interview (or observation) may be seen, however, as "data" and a "theme" in its own right. The interviewer, therefore, always has to keep in mind the question, "Have I heard, interviewed someone, observed an occasion, or seen documents that suggest that this specific piece of data can be trusted?" This goes for the simplest piece of data. For example, perhaps the committee usually has twelve members, and the reasons as to why this verbatim claims that it has eight members, if indeed that is the claim, might be a core theme that is critical to the student's project. Data from journals, field notes, documents, etc., must also be judged in similar fashion.

When data is emerging from a verbatim and is being "coded" and "judged," it helps the researcher to engage in an ongoing critical assessment at the edge of the data's meaning. What hasn't been said? What open-ended questions ought to occur? Who should be interviewed a second or third time? Should a special place, person, or program be observed? Push yourself in the making of such assessments. Try out your hunches with folk you trust; play with peculiar phrases that you pick up. Ask yourself if there are metaphors, analogies, or jargon you have heard that could provide headings for the case study. Follow them up. In other words, find out what is going on in this ministry. For example, Anne Abernethy, in writing on "When the Minister Has a Baby" (noted in chapter seven), was ultimately able to offer a metaphoric structure for the movements within her case study (her final "narrative description") that clearly emerged out of the themes generated by that ministry.

Structure for the Paper

by Anne Abernethy

Introduction (or conception and gestation)
Personal issues (or the birth process)
Family issues (or the new baby comes home)
Theological issues (or baptism, naming God's child)

*   *   *

In other words, at the earliest possible moment, the D.Min. researcher must interactively assess the data generated by the ministry project and begin to write (or at least to put down on paper) some of the thematic "hunches" that might either tell the story of this "practice of ministry" or provide a framework for the resultant story.

Those who use the word processor might recognize the "garbage bag" kind of approach utilized by that technology as another way to name this process of sorting through "apples" and "oranges." Those who use hard copies of notes and interviews without the benefit of a word processor may be forced into a "cut and tape" procedure; i.e., such folk often photocopy the master transcription and then, by using a locator code, clip and place such clippings within the various emerging "apples" and "oranges" categories. For example, I have taped clippings of data cut from journals, field notes, and documents upon walls and tables onto which I also had taped several specific themes ("the mall," "youth fellowship," "liberals," etc.). This had to occur in a very large room. And once cut and taped upon the walls, I was glad to have worked out and written on each piece of paper a "locator code" so that I always could return to the original document, interview, or field note. In either case (word processor, or "cut and tape"), it takes a great deal of organizing effort to reduce the mounds of paper (my "data") to a coherent package (a "case study").

The D.Min. student who is engaged in case-study research and is coding data through this process judges what ought to be included and at the same time, works toward validity by following the principle of triangulation. That is, when data of a similar sort appears through the use of three or more separate research tools (for example, a questionnaire, specific field notes, and a personal journal), the researcher can accept that what is emerging is what is actually present in the ministry being observed and can also affirm that it will stand as believable data. "Validity," therefore, has to do with seeing in the final narrative description (the case study) that which actually was present in the ministry setting. And, if the D.Min. student intends to follow the method "with rigor," emerging themes ought to be confirmed or rejected by feedback drawn either from (a) individuals, i.e., a supervisor, a "key informant," a selected expert, or (b) a purposively chosen panel or group who similarly engage in a friendly critique.

The Presentation of Data

As the D.Min. project, its evaluation, and the author's theoretical stance concerning a problem in the practice of ministry come together in a case study, the author must decide how and when to present data. The examples included in this book were drawn from D.Min. papers whose authors spent considerable time wrestling with this issue. While some opted for a writing style that avoids quantitative bar graphs and other similar displays, still others were comfortable including such presentations of data within the main body of their texts. No matter how data of this sort is presented, however, the case study has to be concerned with how the reader gets attracted, "hooked," or involved with the plot-line of what amounts to a story. Case studies are always narrative descriptions about specific practices of ministry and problems that such ministerial practice is trying to address. This means that "story"with plot, characters, crisis, reversal, and resolution--can and should occur in D.Min. papers. Data therefore gets organized within a framework of themes/major ideas that work toward presenting a story.

The D.Min. paper is also for the practice of ministry with professional peers, and therefore ought to communicate this story to a known audience (pastoral counselors, preachers, religious educators, etc.) in a style and a length that makes sense for that audience. Because of this perspective, overlong and seemingly obtuse D.Min. papers won't work. Ministers therefore ought to be encouraged to "tell the story" of their D.Min. projects in appropriate ways. This is why they have received theological education that includes, among other things, careful attention to the study of hermeneutics. But different D.Min. programs translate these issues in different ways. For example, the program at Chicago Theological Seminary mandates that the final D.Min. paper cannot exceed twenty-five pages and must have a style oriented to the audience of a specific journal. Students in this program are often encouraged to use the following chart as a way to consider the "weighty" task of writing such a case study.

Weighting the Professional Paper

A. 1-2 pages. An eye-catching *introduction* stating a specific problem in the practice of ministry....

B. 2-6 pages. The *theory* used to inform the way(s) a resulting practice of ministry will be implemented....

C. 2-4 pages. The *project* that frames this practice of ministry....

D. 1-2 pages. The *research method* and resultant *tools* used in the evaluation of the project in ministry....

E. 5-10 pages. A descriptive *picture, analysis, and assessment* of the project....

F. 5-10 pages. The *hunches, emerging themes or key insights* gained that might help one's peers....

G. 1-3 pages. A thoughtful *conclusion* including a small, annotated *bibliography.*

*   *   *

From the examples shared in this book, it is clear that the Doctor of Ministry process resists being reduced to a formula; nevertheless, such a descriptive "weighting" of the D.Min. paper causes helpful reflection for most D.Min. students. As such, it can push that student who avoids questions of scope and balance into some semblance of coherence. Creative storytellers, on the other hand, provide scope and balance even when they begin with "G" in the above chart and work backward to "A." And that is why a solid critical reflection on a problem in the practice of ministry always occurs within a readable paper.

Summary

It would appear that the core of what most D.Min. students have to offer--their "good news"--emerges in a case study (that is, a story) through an ongoing discussion and critical reflection that engages theory, the ministry, the project, the data, the student's peers and the wider disciplines of the world. Storytelling, that is, the ability to sense direction in these matters, is very much at the spiritual center and heart of the D.Min. process. "Coding" and "presenting data" is not a mechanical act; it is exactly in this storytelling process that one senses God's presence.

ANNOTATED BIBLIOGRAPHY

1. Paul Atkinson. *The Ethnographic Imagination*. New York: Routledge, 1990. Method: ethnographic. Narrative, voice, irony, and character. . .in what way is the ethnographic *text* a particular literary genre and how does it emerge from both its epistemological and methodological warrants? By affirming that texts are never neutral, Atkinson here sets out to explore how numerous ethnographic texts "achieve their representations of social/sociological reality" (p. 7). How we "read" a text as well as how an author "writes" a text is the subject of this cross-disciplinary work.

2. Earl Babbie. *The Practice of Social Research*. 5th edition. Belmont, Calif.: Wadsworth, 1983. Method: multiple. Describing theoretical principles of research, detailing established tools/approaches for doing research, and engaging the reader in concrete examples of research, Babbie's book is the university student's basic introductory text for social science research. Helpful orientation is provided for five "modes of observation" (methods): (1) experiments, (2) survey research, (3) field research, (4) unobtrusive research, and (5) evaluation research. Questionnaires and interviews are covered under "Survey Research"; sampling and field notes are under "Field Research." Two excellent chapters on "The Ethics and Politics of Social Research" and "The Uses of Social Research" conclude the book. The D.Min. student would read this to become clearer regarding the use and misuse of certain research tools.

3. Judith Bell. *Doing Your Research Project*. 5th edition. Buckingham, Great Britain: Open University Press, 1992. Method: action research. This is a good book to use in a class with D.Min. students. One hundred forty-five pages negotiate the very pragmatic issues of planning the project, reviewing the literature, keeping records, getting into the setting, analyzing documents, using questionnaires, conducting interviews, using a diary, engaging in observation, critical analyses, and writing the end paper. This should be read as a source of reference and a guide to good practice for all beginner researchers.

4. Warren R. Bentzen. *Seeing Young Children: A Guide to Observing and Recording Behavior*. Albany, N.Y.: Delmar, 1985. Method: field observation. The first half of this book presents a clear framework for observing and recording behavior in young children. As such, it defines "open" and "closed" approaches, specimen records, time sampling, event sampling, diary usage, anecdotal recordkeeping, duration and frequency counts, while also providing examples of how these things can happen in given contexts. The second half provides developmental descriptions of the preschool-aged child. Read this book if you want to consider the variety of observational approaches available to the researcher.

5. Anne M. Boylan. *Sunday School: The Formation of an American Institution, 1790-1880.* New Haven: Yale University Press, 1988. Method: historical/documentary. Demonstrating how historic documents can be used to "tell a story," in this instance the emergence of the Sunday School movement within the United States, Boylan intersperses public posters, church bulletins and architectural drawings with a variety of other documents throughout this text. Read this book if you have questions about defining a historic context or using documents within a D.Min. paper.

6. W. Jackson Carroll, Carl S. Dudley, and William McKinney, eds. *Handbook for Congregational Studies.* Nashville: Abingdon Press, 1987. Method: eclectic, but implicitly quantitative. The book's strength rests with its description of a variety of evaluative strategies. These tools appropriately are clustered within four chapters on congregational (a) identity, (b) context, (c) process, and (d) program. Each chapter is from a different author, and the method section is brief. Read this book if you need to find explicit examples of evaluative tools, but couple the selection of such tools with a critical understanding of the implications of method for the D.Min. process.

7. Elliot W. Eisner. *The Enlightened Eye: Qualitative Research and the Enhancement of Educational Practice.* New York: Macmillan, 1991. Method: qualitative. This is an elegant book written about the deeper meaning of method in qualitative inquiry. Eisner writes: "Detachment and distance are no virtues when one wants to improve complex social organizations or so delicate a performance as teaching" (p. 2). An excellent chapter is entitled, "Do Qualitative Case Studies Have Lessons to Teach?" (chap. 9). Read this book for one person's critical perception regarding the quantitative/qualitative discussion.

8. Corrine Glesne and Alan Peshkin. *Becoming Qualitative Researchers: An Introduction.* White Plains, N.Y.: Longman, 1992. Method: qualitative. This is an excellent overview that includes solid pre-study advice as well as intelligent chapters on participant-observation, interviewing, field note taking, and the ethics of it all. There are also excellent chapters on "finding your story" (data analysis), and on "writing your story" (what data means). A brief comment is included on using computers in qualitative research. Good examples of data presentation are interspersed in an introductory overview of the case study process.

9. Pamela L. Grossman. *The Making of A Teacher: Teacher Knowledge and Teacher Education.* New York: Teachers College Press, 1980. Method: comparative case study. Six first-year high school English teachers are characterized in this richly textured picture centered on what it is that they use to guide their teaching. At the same time, Grossman interweaves throughout a working concept of how teachers arrive at their own personal pedagogy. By purposely choosing teachers with and without professional education training, Grossman

provides us with a comparative picture elegant in its simplicity while suggestive to anyone interested in teaching. Grossman's insights ring true, and the D.Min. researcher can profit from both the simplicity of her design and the deft handling of theory.

10. Egon Guba and Yvonna S. Lincoln. *Effective Evaluation*. San Francisco: Jossey Bass, 1981. Method: qualitative. Calling qualitative research a "naturalistic paradigm" standing in contrast to quantitative research (or the "scientific paradigm"), Guba and Lincoln detail their argument in Part I. In Part II they present the "naturalistic method of inquiry." The D.Min. student can make use of their excellent summaries on interviews, observation, documents, and unobtrusive procedures, as well as their clear description on how a case study can be used to present critical analysis of a project. Read this book for the philosophic argument (Part I) and pragmatic advice on doing case-study research (Part II).

11. Martyn Hammersley and Paul Atkinson. *Ethnography Principles in Practice*. New York: Tavistock, 1983. Method: ethnography. Hammersley and Atkinson give us a well-written appraisal of the range of tools, strategies, and issues confronting the ethnographer. This is one of the clearest and most helpful texts available on ethnography. Read it for both theory and example, but if you have questions about how the researcher is an "active participant" and can become "the research instrument *par excellence*" (p. 18), this is the book.

12. Richard M. Jaeger, ed. *Complementary Methods for Research in Education*. Washington: American Educational Research Association, 1988. Method: multiple. Presenting a broad sweep of historic, philosophical, ethnographic, survey, comparative, and quasi-experimental methods often used by educational researchers, this book is companioned by a set of audio tapes and a printed study guide.. A D.Min. student or adviser might read this book to catch the wide-ranging methodological approaches available to the contemporary researcher.

13. Danny L. Jorgensen. *Participant Observation: A Methodology for Human Studies*. Newbury Park, Calif.: Sage Publications, 1989. Method: qualitative/ethnography. Written for the budding qualitative researcher in the social sciences, this text describes in clear, straightforward fashion how "outsiders" can begin to understand what Jorgensen calls a "humanistic methodology" (p. 7), enter research settings, and collect, code, and analyze data. Read this book if you seek a simple (yet not simplistic) overview of ethnography or pro-active research.

14. Catherine Marshall and Gretchen B. Rossman. *Designing Qualitative Research*. Newbury Park, California: Sage Publications, Inc., 1989. Method: qualitative. Packed with twenty-four "vignettes" of published qualitative research, this book is simple (without being simplistic) and would be an important companion to *Research in Ministry*. The strength of the book lies in how well the authors carefully marshall appropriate vignettes illustrating each point

of their theoretical framework. In addition, excellent suggestions are made regarding a variety of primary data collection techniques, including: observation, interviewing, questionnaires and surveys, films, photographs, video tapes, projective techniques, proxemics (use of space), kinesics (body movement), street ethnography, historical analysis, life history, content analyses, and unobtrusive measures.

15. James H. McMillan and Sally Schumacher. *Research in Education*. Boston: Little, Brown, 1984. Method: multiple. A standard textbook, *Research in Education* covers in careful detail both quantitative and qualitative research methods. Good introductions are included regarding questionnaires, interviews, field observations, and unobtrusive measures. Excellent chapters are also included in "Ethnographic Research" and "Literature Review." There are also usable summaries of inferential statistics and historical studies. Read this book if you seek an overview regarding method or a second opinion, for example, about sampling or designing a questionnaire.

16. Sharan B. Merriam. *Case Study Research in Education: A Qualitative Approach*. San Francisco: Jossey-Bass, 1991. Method: case study. Merriam gives a straightforward account of what defines a case study, what goes into building a case study, and why this process is of value. Easily read, this book is pragmatic regarding how to collect data, and it provides two full chapters on data analysis. The issues of validity, reliability, and ethics are also covered. Read this book if you want a clear description of the process and the product known as "case study."

17. Duane R. Monette, Thomas J. Sullivan, and Cornell R. DeJong. *Applied Social Research: Tool for the Human Sciences*. New York: Holt, Rinehart and Winston, 1986. Method: multiple. This is a social worker's introductory research text. As such, it provides detailed information about the construction of questionnaires, sampling procedures, and interviewing techniques, as well as how to "do" field notes and content analysis. This book could be read both by the professor who wants to know, in detail, about "applied social research," and by the student who wants to learn a pragmatic approach to research "tools."

18. William R. Myers. *Black and White Styles of Youth Ministry: Two Congregations in America*. New York: Pilgrim Press, 1991. Method: comparative case study. Using field notes, interviews, documents, a personal journal, and the procedures discussed in this primer on research, *Black and White Styles* compares the youth ministry of a purposively-chosen African-American U.C.C. congregation with that of a youth ministry in a Presbyterian Church (U.S.A.) white congregation. Educational agendas emerge, and a historic framework is used to interpret why the African-American church is more explicit in agenda than is the Eurocentric congregation. Read this book if you want to understand how the suggestions of *Research in Ministry* take place in the critical evaluation of a "practice of ministry."

19. Michael Quinn Patton. *Qualitative Evaluation and Research Methods, Second Edition*. Newbury Park, California: Sage Publications, Inc. 1990. Method: qualitative. Patton presents his classic (and basic) book. Both lucid and helpful, it is arranged in three sections: (1) conceptual issues; (2) qualitative design and data collection; (3) analyses, interpretation and reporting. "Naturalistic observation takes place in the field," Patton observes, and then spells out the distinct advantages of such direct observation. His open, discovery-oriented, inductive methodology helps the researcher see things routinely missed or "selectively edited" by staff and participants from any given program or site. An excellent resource for someone needing a solid theoretical and pragmatic approach to qualitative evaluation and research.

20. W. James Popham and Kenneth A. Sirotnik. *Understanding Statistics in Education*. Itasca, Ill: F. E. Peacock, 1992. Method: quantitative/statistical. This is the one book included that offers a clear overview of the quantitative approach to statistical research. If you want to understand "Analysis of Covariance" or "Chi Square Tests," this is a good place to begin. Read this book if quantitative research is important within your D.Min. course of study.

21. Arthur G. Powell, Eleanor Farrar, and David K. Cohen. *The Shopping Mall High School: Winners and Losers in the Educational Marketplace*. Boston: Houghton Mifflin, 1985. Method: case study. Commissioned as the second book to emerge from a five-year inquiry into secondary education (A Study of High Schools) by the National Association of Secondary School Principals, and the Commission on Educational Issues of the National Association of Independent Schools, this book is an example of team research and collaborative writing using field notes, interviews, and documents. Note that the research apparatus is submerged. This book should be read if you are interested in understanding how data can be used to structure story.

22. Virginia E. Schein. *Working From the Margins: Voices of Mothers in Poverty*. Ithaca, New York: ILR Press — an imprint of Cornell University Press, 1995. Method: comparative case study. Thirty women tell Schein their stories. By pursuing a "contextual approach" to each story, Schein brings front and center individual, historical, and societal factors. The generative themes emerging from this approach give rise to provocative *metaphors* (one chapter is entitled "Stone Soup: Parenting in Poverty") as well as *narrative* flow. I include Schein's book as an excellent example of the pro-active style of research presented in *Research in Ministry*. I think most good D.Min. papers are quite similar to Schein's work.

23. William H. Schubert and William C. Ayers. *Teacher Lore: Learning From Our Own Experience*. New York: Longman Publishing Group, 1992. Method: participant observation. Schubert and Ayers firmly believe that teachers both understand and know best what it means "to teach." This edited volume bears out the truth of that simple insight. Along the way, it serves up a rich pottage

of diaries, remembering essays, fictional insights, and personal journals. While the essays are by individual authors, on every page one senses the dialogue of a larger community of scholars. I include this book in order to suggest that the activity of *research* is a much more normal activity than is often perceived by ministers.

24. James P. Spradley. *Participant Observation*. Chicago: Holt, Rinehart and Winston, 1960. Method: ethnographic. Spradley gives the student a step-by-step procedure "to begin research, collect data, analyze what you find, and write up your report." While Spradley writes for the beginning ethnographer, much of what he details can be helpful for the person engaged in research in ministry. Note that he is interested in making an analysis of a given culture, and that some of his principles are anchored in "domain analysis" of a particular sort. Both this book and Spradley's *The Ethnographic Interview* (Chicago: Holt, Rinehart and Winston, 1979) are helpful, but *Participant Observation* includes much of what he then amplifies in *The Ethnographic Interview*. Read *Participant Observation* if you want to have a sense of the necessary steps an ethnographer must take.

25. Melinda Bollar Wagner. *God's Schools: Choice and Compromise in American Society*. New Brunswick, N.J.: Rutgers University Press, 1990. Method: ethnographic. A careful ethnography of nine Christian schools in "southeastern valley," Wagner's work interweaves verbatims, field notes, personal observations, documents, and demographic data within a readable, engaging story. Every quote in this text is followed by a reference to data. I enclose this book because of its clear presentation of data. An appendix concerning her method is very helpful (pp. 217-232). Read this book if you have questions about the explicit presentation of data within a text.

26. R. Stephen Warner. *New Wine in Old Wineskins: Evangelicals and Liberals in a Small-Town Church*. Berkeley: University of California Press, 1988. Method: ethnographic. Sociologist Warner sets the historic framework, enters one California Presbyterian Church (U.S.A.) congregation, and details that congregation's change within a critically-reflective interpretation. Documents, interviews, field notes, demographic data, and the "self as instrument" are made readily apparent in the text, as is a clear bibliographic grasp of secondary and philosophic documents. Read it if you want to see how the reflexive process of ethnography results in a fine study of a congregation in turmoil by a first-rate "observer-participant."

NOTES ABOUT THE CONTRIBUTORS

Examples used in this book were taken from Doctor of Ministry papers published by Exploration Press of the Chicago Theological Seminary, 5757 S. University Ave., Chicago, Illinois 60637. At the time of their paper's publication, contributors identified themselves in the following manner.

Anne B. Abernethy is affiliated with the United Church of Christ and is currently serving as pastor of the First Congregational Church, U.C.C., Berwyn, Illinois. She is a graduate of Davidson College and received an M.Div. degree from the University of Dubuque Theological Seminary, an M.A. degree from the Aquinas Institute of Theology, and a D.Min. degree from the Chicago Theological Seminary.

Ann Bartram teaches pastoral counseling at the Toronto School of Theology and is Director of Training at the Toronto Institute of Human Relations. She is a graduate of the University of Western Ontario. She received her B.D. from Victoria University and her D.Min. from the Chicago Theological Seminary.

Thomas J. Byrne, a member of the Holy Ghost Fathers order, is currently Associate Professor of Pastoral Theology and Field Education at the University of St. Thomas School of Theology, in Houston, Texas. He received B.A. and B.Th. degrees from the University of Connecticut, an M.Div. degree from the Oblate School of Theology, and a D.Min. degree from the Chicago Theological Seminary.

John Chalmers will be Director for Pastoral Formation at Pius XII Seminary, Australia, and the Brisbane School of Theology as of February 1992. He received his B.A. and B.Th. equivalent from Pius XII Seminary, Banyo, Australia, an M.A. degree from Loyola University of Chicago, and a D.Min. degree from the Chicago Theological Seminary. He is currently working on a Th.M. focusing on pastoral theology at Candler School of Theology, Emory University.

Avis Clendenen is currently the Assistant Professor of Religious Studies and Director of the Pastoral Ministry Institute at Saint Xavier University. A graduate of Saint Xavier College, she received an M.Div. degree from the Jesuit School of Theology at Chicago, and D.Min. and Ph.D. degrees from the Chicago Theological Seminary.

The late **Maria C. Gabriel** earned a B.A. degree from the University of Miami. She received an M.T.S. degree from the Catholic Theological Union (Chicago), and a D.Min. from the Chicago Theological Seminary.

Gary S. Gerson is Rabbi of the Oak Park Temple B'nai Abraham Zion. He received a B.A. from the University of Michigan, an M.A. in religion, and an M.A. in psychology from Temple University, and a D.Min. from the Chicago Theological Seminary.

Thomas M. Holden, S.J. is on the staff of the Family Care Network of Christ Hospital, Oak Lawn, Illinois. His clinical training as a pastoral counselor was at the Pastoral Psychotherapy Institute of Lutheran General Hospital. He is a Jesuit priest who studied philosophy and psychology at Loyola University of Chicago and theology at the Gregorian University in Rome. He received his D.Min. from the Chicago Theological Seminary.

Amy Therese Kenealy, SSSF, a member of the School Sisters of St. Francis, is pastoral associate at St. Joachim Church, Chicago, Illinois, and a program director of the Pastoral Ministry Institute, St. Xavier College. She holds the following degrees: a B.A. from Alverno College, an M.A. from the University of Chicago, a C.A.S. from the University of Illinois (Urbana), an M.S. from Chicago State University, an M.A. from St. Mary of the Woods College, and a D.Min. from the Chicago Theological Seminary.

Richard Kirchherr is an Associate Pastor of the First Congregational Church, U.C.C. of Western Springs. His B.A. was received from the University of Illinois at the Champaign-Urbana campus. An M.Div. graduate of the Chicago Theological Seminary, he also holds a D.Min. from that institution done with faculty in the Chicago D.Min. in Preaching Program.

Bonnie J. Niswander is coordinator of Pastoral Psychotherapy Training of the Pastoral Psychotherapy Institute, which is affiliated with Lutheran General Medical Center in Park Ridge, Illinois. She is a fellow of the American Association of Pastoral Counselors, and a member of the Advisory Council of the Institute for Religion and Wholeness, Claremont, California. She received her B.A. from Ohio Wesleyan University and her D.Min. from the Chicago Theological Seminary.

James O'Connell is a student counselor in the House of Studies of the Mill Hill Missionary Society at St. Joseph's College, London. He holds a B.A. from the National University of Ireland, an S.T.L. from the Gregorian University in Rome, and a D.Min. from the Chicago Theological Seminary.

Lynne Schmidt is a staff member of the Ecumenical Center at the University of Louisville. She has served for six years as an associate pastor in Missouri, Nebraska, and Honduras, and for nine years as a secondary teacher of religion and English in Missouri and California. She is a member of the School Sisters of Notre Dame. She received her B.A. degree from Notre Dame College, her M.A. degree from Ball State University, her M.Div. from the Catholic Theological Union, and her D.Min. from the Chicago Theological Seminary.

Dale H. Schumm is Director of Personnel for the Mennonite Board of Missions. Previously he served as Director for Admissions for the Associated Mennonite Biblical Seminaries in Elkhart, Indiana, missionary to India, and pastor in the Mennonite Church in Ontario. He holds a B.A. from Eastern Mennonite College, a B.D. from Goshen Biblical Seminary, an M.Div. from Associated Mennonite Biblical Seminaries, and a D.Min. from the Chicago Theological Seminary.

C. Michael Smith is a minister of the Disciples of Christ and is currently Executive Director and pastoral psychotherapist at the Haelan Counseling and Psychology Center, Niles, Michigan. He received a B.A. degree from Indiana Christian University, M.A.R. and M.Div. degrees from Christian Theological Seminary, and D.Min. and Ph.D. degrees from the Chicago Theological Seminary.

Felix Sugirtharaj is engaged in educational and church work in India. He holds a B.A. from the University of Madras, a Diploma in Theology from United Theological College (India), an M.S.T. from Union Theological Seminary (New York), and a D.Min. from the Chicago Theological Seminary.